TSUNAMI

TSUNAMI

WOMEN'S VOICES
FROM MEXICO

EDITED BY
Heather Cleary and Gabriela Jauregui

TRANSLATED FROM THE SPANISH BY
Heather Cleary, Gabriela Jauregui,
Julianna Neuhouser, Gabriela Ramirez-Chavez,
and Julia Sanches

THE FEMINIST PRESS
AT THE CITY UNIVERSITY OF NEW YORK
NEW YORK CITY

Published in 2025 by the Feminist Press
at the City University of New York
The Graduate Center
365 Fifth Avenue, Suite 5406
New York, NY 10016

feministpress.org

First Feminist Press edition 2025

Compilation and introduction copyright © 2025 by Gabriela Jauregui and Heather Cleary
Translation copyright © 2025 by Heather Cleary, Gabriela Jauregui, Julianna Neuhouser, Gabriela Ramirez-Chavez, and Julia Sanches
Individual copyright retained by the respective contributors. Additional copyright information appears on page 305, which constitutes a continuation of this copyright page.
Tsunami, *Tsunami 2*, and *Tsunami 3* were originally published in 2018, 2020, and 2024 by Sexto Piso, Mexico

All rights reserved.

This book is made possible by the New York State Council on the Arts with the support of the Office of the Governor and the New York State Legislature.

This book is supported in part by an award from the National Endowment for the Arts.

No part of this book may be reproduced, used, or stored in any information retrieval system or transmitted in any form or by any means, electronic, mechanical, photocopying, recording, or otherwise, without prior written permission from the Feminist Press at the City University of New York, except in the case of brief quotations embodied in critical articles and reviews.

First printing February 2025

Cover design by Sukruti Anah Staneley
Cover illustration by Pia Camil
Text design by Drew Stevens

Library of Congress Cataloging-in-Publication Data
Names: Cleary, Heather, editor, translator. | Jauregui, Gabriela, editor, translator. | Sanches, Julia, translator. | Ramirez-Chavez, Gabriela, translator. | Neuhouser, Julianna, 1987- translator.
Title: Tsunami : women's voices from Mexico / edited by Heather Cleary and Gabriela Jauregui ; translated from the Spanish by Heather Cleary, Julia Sanches, Gabriela Ramirez-Chavez, Julianna Neuhouser, and Gabriela Jauregui.
Description: First Feminist Press edition. | New York City : The Feminist Press at the City University of New York, 2025.
Identifiers: LCCN 2024039233 (print) | LCCN 2024039234 (ebook) | ISBN 9781558613270 (paperback) | ISBN 9781558613294 (ebook)
Subjects: LCSH: Feminism--Mexico. | Women's rights. | LCGFT: Creative nonfiction.
Classification: LCC HQ1155 .T7813 2025 (print) | LCC HQ1155 (ebook) | DDC 305.4209--dc23/eng/20240906
LC record available at https://lccn.loc.gov/2024039233
LC ebook record available at https://lccn.loc.gov/2024039234

PRINTED IN THE UNITED STATES OF AMERICA

CONTENTS

ix PREFACE
Heather Cleary and Gabriela Jauregui

1 BLOOD, LANGUAGE, SURNAME:
INDIGENOUS WOMEN AND NATION-STATES
Yásnaya Elena A. Gil // tr. Gabriela Ramirez-Chavez

17 REBELLION OF THE CASSANDRAS
Marina Azahua // tr. Julia Sanches

41 HEARTQUAKES: AN EMOTIONAL
GEOGRAPHY
Fernanda Latani M. Bravo //
tr. Gabriela Ramirez-Chavez

53 FEMINISM WITHOUT A ROOM OF
ONE'S OWN
Dahlia de la Cerda // tr. Julianna Neuhouser

97 PRESERVING TRANS HISTORY
Alexandra R. DeRuiz // tr. Heather Cleary

CONTENTS

109 TO SEA CHANGE: METAPHORS OF
TRANS' PAIN
Lia García, La Novia Sirena //
tr. Gabriela Ramirez-Chavez

125 THE OTHERS
Jimena González // tr. Gabriela Jauregui

131 DISOBEDIENT TOOLS
Gabriela Jauregui // tr. Julianna Neuhouser

145 BLACK WATER
Valeria Luiselli

165 I AM HUNGER
Ytzel Maya // tr. Julia Sanches

185 4 AND A HALF DIATRIBES IN MEXICO CITY
Brenda Navarro //
tr. Heather Cleary and Gabriela Jauregui

197 THE STORIES WE ARE MADE OF
Jumko Ogata-Aguilar // tr. Julianna Neuhouser

213 WHILE THE GIRLS ARE ASLEEP
Daniela Rea // tr. Gabriela Ramirez-Chavez

253 FIRST PERSON PLURAL
Cristina Rivera Garza // tr. Heather Cleary

CONTENTS

269 MEDAL OR STIGMA
Diana J. Torres // tr. Heather Cleary

281 ALONE
Sara Uribe // tr. Heather Cleary

295 LETTER FROM THE ZAPATISTA WOMEN TO WOMEN IN STRUGGLE AROUND THE WORLD
Zapatista Army for National Liberation (EZLN)

305 PERMISSIONS ACKNOWLEDGMENTS

309 ABOUT THE CONTRIBUTORS

PREFACE

SINCE 2018, the essays and poems contained in *Tsunami* have moved readers in Mexico and throughout Latin America. These texts have witnessed and energized our struggles. They have kept us company. The first volume focused on multiple forms of violences—combating, resignifying, transforming, and naming how violence is inscribed in the body and the world—while the second expanded the wave to include questions about who we are and how to rethink our identities as a starting point (rather than the endpoint) of diverse but interconnected forms of resistance. The third volume, published in 2024, deals primarily with the body-territory continuum and its many forms of defense. A selection from the first two volumes and a preview of the third is included here in translation for the first time. *Tsunami* is now resignified, transformed. Yours.

The essays and poems selected for the English edition of *Tsunami* seek to de-center hegemonic white feminism and to open spaces where different experiences of womanhood and political engagement can resonate with one another in generative conversation. Offering a sense of the diverse voices resisting patriarchy and its embedded structures in Mexico today, voices from within and outside academic institutions,

Trans* voices, Indigenous voices, Afro-Latinx voices, established and emerging voices from generations spanning the entire twentieth century participate in this invocation, provocation, and invitation.

The title of the collection asserts this plurality: *Tsunami* is the combined force of the three feminist waves, the marea verde (green wave) of protests that swept through Latin America, culminating in the legalization of abortion in several countries and states, and the waves made by women whose theory and praxis resist from the margins of hegemonic discourse. The volumes of *Tsunami* from which this anthology draws were published in Mexico against the backdrop of an emerging #MeToo movement, massive and sustained protests across the country, and a seemingly endless stream of news stories about gender-based violence. This context is palpable on every page, in essays that portray a society at once richly diverse and profoundly vertical; a society in which collectives *do* make a difference, but where these prove essential in the absence of state support or—often—in the presence of state violence. Within this specificity, these accounts and philosophies are inextricably intertwined with the experience of prejudice and marginalization in the United States, just as the histories, languages, and cultures of Mexico and the United States have long been intertwined.

These are writings on feminism, rather than feminist writings: many contributors take a critical stance toward the colonial roots of white feminism and explain its limitations in clear, compelling language. Likewise, the formats and registers of the texts are as diverse as their authors, several of whom choose to organize their work in ways that might seem more familiar to readers of scholarship in English, whereas others write in the long and illustrious Latin American tradition of the conversational essay. Several authors in the collection have no interest in, or actively resist, conforming to elitist style guidelines. We made the political and editorial choice—with the support of the team at Feminist Press—to preserve these diverse approaches, opting for polyvocality instead of homogenizing their different textures. Rather than imposing consistency across the anthology in order to conform to norms, we choose to celebrate the many forms critical political thought can take.

Following the Mexican volumes, we organized this *Tsunami* in alphabetical order by author in order to allow for unexpected resonances, but the texts do lend themselves to certain conceptual groupings. For example, several of these essays look back in time to make sense of the present. Shuttling back and forth to connect Greek mythology with the massive women's march that took place in Mexico City in 2019 and other recent events, Marina Azahua's "Rebellion of the Cassandras" is a declaration of the many forms of violence enacted upon women and the power of being heard by others, while Cristina Rivera Garza's "First Person Plural" engages thinkers from Virginia Woolf to Claudia Rankine and Sara Ahmed to examine the affective bonds and the myriad forms of paid and unpaid labor that go into constructing our communities, insisting on the hidden collectivity behind that coveted "room of one's own." Dahlia de la Cerda's incandescent contribution takes an even more critical stance toward Woolf's famous essay, insisting on how inextricably race-class privilege is tied to the production and legitimation of knowledge; and in "Preserving Trans History," Alexandra R. DeRuiz brings us back to Mexico City from the 1960s through the 1980s to visibilize the luminous communities and collective forms of resistance to the repression of sexual dissidence that paved the way for LGBTTTQIA+ movements today.

Another constellation of texts touches on the theme of maternity in diverse ways, many of which are tinged with violence. Jimena González's poem "The Others" vindicates a woman's right to feel desire, to speak out, and to experience pleasure as it catalogs the marginalization and abuse of the women in the author's family; while in her deeply personal essay "Alone," the poet Sara Uribe takes as a point of departure the abuse she endured as a child and her decision to live the last years of her adolescence under the radar of the state because it was safer than being absorbed into its network of orphanages and foster homes. "While the Girls Are Asleep," Daniela Rea's essay in the form of a diary, which she kept over the course of four years and the birth of her two daughters, presents lyrical and brutally honest reflections on the joys, challenges, and fears of being a mother, particularly when dealing with a child's illness. The threads running through Brenda Navarro's "4 and a Half Diatribes in Mexico City" include kinship, class, and the cynical performance of allyship.

Other essays center questions surrounding sexuality, gender, and the ways bodies are read and policed. In "Medal or Stigma," Diana J. Torres reflects on the time she was stabbed in the leg during a robbery, and how the violence of that encounter intersects with other forms of violence that allow her to move more freely because her body is not read as "female" according to hegemonic gender norms. "I Am Hunger" is a potent lyrical essay that explores the relationship between language, body, and power; how the definitions author Ytzel Maya was taught for words like "girl," "whore," and "gay" determined—or tried to

PREFACE xiii

determine—the horizons of her world, and how the delegitimation of words like "lesbifemicide" suppresses the struggle for visibility and justice. In "To Sea Change: Metaphors of Trans' Pain," an exquisitely crafted essay that flows between its central themes like the tide, Lia García, La Novia Sirena (The Mermaid Bride) explores how water has played a fundamental role in her understanding of her body, from the experience of diving into a river as "a girl living in the body of a sad and confused boy" to her love of pearls—the beauty produced by the oyster in response to a wound.

Language itself, and the histories it constructs, are also the subject of critical inquiry. Following Audre Lorde, in "Disobedient Tools," Gabriela Jauregui asks what tools we can forge to combat patriarchy—since those of the master will never dismantle the master's house—and how we can speak from spaces that do not reproduce the same hierarchies and dynamics we seek to overturn. With her characteristic precision and elegance, in "Blood, Language, Surname" Yásnaya Elena A. Gil interrogates the structures of belonging and exclusion produced by language through an analysis of the words "feminism" and "indigenous," terms that mark identity, community, and the rights (or lack thereof) that attend them. Meanwhile, Jumko Ogata-Aguilar's "The Stories We Are Made Of" reflects on the way personal narratives create not only an individual sense of identity, but also a sense of communal belonging, and how the language we use shapes what is considered "exotic" and what counts—or does not—as history.

The deep connection between the body and the natural world is also a subject of reflection. Valeria Luiselli's "Black Water" (originally written in English as part of a sound piece on violence against bodies and the environment in the borderlands) examines, in the form of a Greek tragedy, the interconnected themes of plunder—of land, labor, and women's bodies—and violence—both environmental and sexual. Likewise, in "Heartquakes: An Emotional Geography," Fernanda Latani M. Bravo draws connections between the seismic shifts that disrupt, or end, lives—like the 8.2 magnitude earthquake that devastated Oaxaca in 2017—and the seismic shifts that take place within each of us at different moments in our lives; in her case, centered around her complicated and painful relationship with her mother.

The final text included in the collection is the "Letter from the Zapatista Women to Women in Struggle Around the World," delivered by Insurgenta Erika in 2018 on behalf of the Zapatista women who composed it collectively. The text reflects the experience of Indigenous women who suffer violence and exploitation for being women, who see their communities starved for resources, healthcare, and education—and who nonetheless find the strength to take up arms. Focusing not only on the violence enacted by men, but also on the ways women (particularly women from the urban elite) undermine the struggles of their sisters, the letter draws strength from diversity and difference to advocate for a unified front against femicide, land theft, and plunder.

In Mexico and Latin America, *Tsunami* became a mirror carried along the road of life—our struggles, celebrations, concerns, and imaginative possibilities reflected in words. For the English edition, we decided to undertake this necessary translation collectively, in the spirit of the original *Tsunami*s and also as part of the process of memory-formation that is essential to building a future. Each of the five translators who worked on the anthology chose their texts based on affinity and participated in workshops to help their peers with drafts, in addition to the editorial support we provided throughout the process.

This iteration of *Tsunami*, then, allows us to imagine our worlds anew. We would like to thank the translators in this collective endeavor for all their extraordinary work, and also to express our gratitude to the authors for entrusting their texts to us, to Lauren Hook for believing in this project, and to Kameel Mir and the whole team at Feminist Press for shepherding this volume into being. We cannot wait to see the new ways these waves of words swell into their new context and language.

—Gabriela Jauregui and Heather Cleary
Mexico City
2024

Yásnaya Elena A. Gil
tr. Gabriela Ramirez-Chavez

BLOOD, LANGUAGE, SURNAME:
INDIGENOUS WOMEN AND
NATION-STATES

WORDS AS QUESTIONS

Learning a second language is an endless process, like the process of acquiring our mother tongue. Mixe is my first language, and I am still learning new words—lexical elements that seem strange to me at first glance but bring to light a new field of cognition and worldview that had previously been clouded by ineffability. The same is true for native Spanish speakers—or is there any Spanish speaker whose mental inventory holds every, absolutely every, word that exists in the language? In colonial and racist contexts, learning a hegemonic second language has complex implications for processes of identity, and learning certain words in that language poses a challenge far beyond proper pronunciation or basic meaning.

Certain words in Spanish have always confronted me with questions about my positionality, about my identity and what it means to be woven into a new lexical network. "Indigenous" and "feminism" were two lexical elements that remained uncomfortable, even after I learned enough about their meanings so as not to confuse them with other words: I did not know how to position myself in relation to them, what they meant, or the social framework in which they were embedded. Their frequent use, much to my dismay, was a constant reminder that my relationship to them was still unresolved.

In many Indigenous languages, as in the case of my mother tongue, there is no equivalent word for "Indigenous." Mixe words referring to non-Mixe groups are mediated by other understandings of difference: to be or not be Mixe, to be ayuujk jä̈äy or to be akäts. The word akäts covers the diverse continuum of not being Mixe—the whole universe of often contrasting people who are not: an Indigenous Sámi person from Norway, a Zapotec person, or an English-speaking Canadian are all akäts, not Mixes. Having grown up at a time and in a place where Spanish did not have a fundamental role, in a community surrounded by other Mixe and Zapotec communities, to me the word "Indigenous" was nothing more than a lexical element spoken by some visiting public official. It wasn't until I arrived in the city that, without intending to, I became "Indigenous" and had to position myself in relation to the term. Every chance I get, I like to tell the story of how my grandmother, a Mixe speaker, denied being Indigenous when asked directly, saying "I am Mixe, not Indigenous." That word never came to her, never interpellated her, in a language she does not speak.

Time has passed since my initial refusal to be categorized as Indigenous and to use the term. Now I relate to the word differently, but I cannot deny that building that relationship was difficult. I understand "Indigenous" as a word that names nations, individuals, and communities that suffered through processes of colonization; since the formation of modern nation-states, Indigenous nations have been forced to exist within these legal entities. These nation-states have fought against the existence of Indigenous nations and relate to them through oppression. Indigenous peoples are nations without a state. I understand now that the word "Indigenous" names a political category, not a cultural or racial one (though

BLOOD, LANGUAGE, SURNAME

it has indeed been racialized). I also understand that it was not enough to reject and not use the word "Indigenous" to stop the category from affecting me. I realized that it is possible to use the word as a political tool to subvert the structures that sustain it despite the ever-present risk of falling into the rivers of folklorization and essentialization.

As for the other word, I cannot yet draw any conclusions. I still find myself dancing around it, anxiously at times. Since I learned it, I have related to it in various ways, ranging from outright rejection to enthusiasm, without taking a definitive stance. Besides being "Indigenous," I am a woman. Patriarchy and patriarchal systems run through me, and feminism seeks to subvert these categories of oppression. There is no way for the word not to interpellate me, even if it calls to me in uncomfortable ways. I soon realized that my complex relationship with feminism is shared by many Indigenous women in the struggle all around the world.

Some believe Indigenous women's struggles should not be equated with feminism or even be called feminism. Others believe they must at least reframe the term in a way that accounts for their own experiences and captures a more complex web of oppressions. In an interview, Quechua activist Tarcila Rivera Zea explains, "It has been difficult for Indigenous women to understand [non-Indigenous] feminism and to understand whether or not we are feminists. So we came to the conclusion that we have to build our own feminism, based on our own references."[1] Listening to various conversations between the Mixe Zapotec activist Sofía Robles and the Mixe political scientist Tajëëw Díaz Robles, I began to understand that

1. For the full interview in Spanish, see https://www.elsaltodiario.com/feminismos/tarcila-rivera-zea-mujeres-indigenas-construir-nuestro-propio-concepto-feminismo.

many Indigenous women share these concerns and respond very differently to "feminism," a concept and word from a colonial language, and the way it constantly interpellates us. We find ourselves in a complex situation, one that challenges us to question feminism without echoing patriarchal perspectives and to prevent our questions from being coopted and used against the feminist movement.

In my search for answers, I found a clear explanation regarding the origin of the difficult relationship between feminism and Indigenous women in the work of Kaqchikel writer Aura Cumes.[2] When it comes to Indigenous women, she argues, the patriarchal system cannot be explained without colonization, and colonization cannot be explained without patriarchal oppression. In this way, gender conditions are created not only in the context of Western patriarchy, but also within a colonial system where power relations are established: in the case of patriarchy, it is about power relations with respect to men, and in the case of colonial domination it is with respect to non-Indigenous women, or Western women. For Cumes, these relations of coloniality with white women take a new form within feminist organizations, where Indigenous women are not treated equally. The discourse within Western feminist spaces often reinforces the idea that Indigenous women's struggles stem from being part of an intrinsically more sexist culture and are therefore a matter "between Indigenous people" that has nothing to do with the colonial system. This colonial system

2. I refer to her doctoral thesis "La 'india' como 'sirvienta': Servidumbre doméstica, colonialismo y patriarcado en Guatemala" (CIESAS, Mexico, 2014) and her article "Multiculturalismo, género y feminismos: Mujeres diversas, luchas complejas" in *Participación y políticas de mujeres indígenas en contextos latinoamericanos recientes*, edited by Andrea Pequeño (FLACSO, Ecuador, 2009).

unites white women and white men through what Cumes calls a "racial pact"—although they are divided by patriarchal relations, they are united by racial privilege. Yet, Cumes emphasizes, it is precisely this intersection of oppressions that makes Indigenous women's struggles and approaches so powerful, so effective at challenging the social order: their voices speak from many sites of oppression, not just one.

Aura Cumes's reflections shaped my understanding and put into words why feminism makes me uncomfortable: it is the colonial relationship that permeates patriarchal relations, it is the colonial asymmetry that mediates my relationship to feminism. If non-Indigenous women have a complex relationship with the meanings and implications of feminism already, then for Indigenous women, the colonial hierarchy radically complicates the situation and explains, I think, their very diverse responses to and ways of interacting with feminism. It is a structural issue.

Considering these ideas, I would like to offer some reflections regarding how Indigenous women respond to this doubly articulated site that mediates our desires, reflections, and responses—both as Indigenous (a political category) and as women (permeated by patriarchal categories), since both aspects are interwoven, not just compounded.

The experiences of Indigenous women, women of flesh and bone, can be understood from a cultural perspective; in this sense, the boundaries of "Indigenous" as a category are blurred, and multiple contrasting identities and cultural specificities emerge. The experience of a Mixe woman from a given community is very different from that of another woman from the Ainu people of Japan or a Sámi woman from Finland. The history and culture of the Mixe people can be traced back thousands of years before colonialism and the formation of nation-states, and we Mixe women are nourished by that history and culture in constant movement and transformation. Were it not for the patriarchy and colonialism of which Cumes writes, our history and culture would have a more central role when we explain and narrate our experience. However, this is not the case. At least, not entirely.

Colonialism, which nation-states have reconfigured and continue to deploy, also brings us together under the category of Indigenous—a political category, as I said above—and that is the basis of resistance. But we also run the risk of essentializing that category as if it were a cultural trait. Culturally, I am Mixe; politically, I am an Indigenous Mixe woman. The risk of assuming the category without calling it into question results in accepting the features and traits that nation-states seek to impose on us. Identifying as Indigenous can, on one hand, mean positioning oneself in political resistance to colonialism and the state, recognizing the struggles of all women who belong to nations without a state as being rooted in the same struggle. On the other hand, when we can call ourselves Indigenous, we might reproduce, not always voluntarily, the narratives of nation-states, which are always depoliticized and folklorizing, and reproduce subjection. These two sides of the relationship we might establish—often involuntarily—produce specific concerns and particular anxieties.

BLOOD

Many years ago, I read about the experience of a First-Nations woman in Canada who wrote about her love life and its drawbacks on her blog, evidencing those concerns and anxieties. The Canadian state uses blood quantum to certify that a person is Indigenous: if the mother and father of a given person belong to a First Nation, this person is said to be 100 percent Indigenous; if only the father is recognized as First Nations, then this person is 50 percent Indigenous, and so on in diminishing percentages. The Canadian state recognizes the rights of First Nations and individuals based on this blood quantum, which has changed over time. Since the nineteenth century, the state began to keep a register of Indigenous people it included and excluded: at that time, if a First-Nations woman married a non-Indigenous man (with legal status), she was excluded from the register and ceased to be First Nations, legally speaking. Up until 1960, if an Indigenous person wanted to vote in elections, they had to renounce their legal status as First Nations.

The implications of and requirements for being considered First Nations have changed over time, but even as the requirements have been relaxed, the state is clearly still in control. In 2016, the Canadian Supreme Court recognized approximately 200,000 Métis with a certain "percentage of native blood" as having First-Nations status. Over time, these legal requirements have become an important part of First-Nations peoples' narratives and, in many cases, First-Nations people reproduce this recognition by the state, which in the end profoundly impacts women's discourses and their experiences of identity. They might define themselves as 100 percent or 50 percent Indigenous, and the number of First-Nations people per tribe seriously impacts the ability to defend their territory and to access their rights. In this context, I can understand how the state's sanctioning of who is and is not Indigenous cuts through something as intimate and personal as the love life of a First-Nations woman in Canada. On her blog, the woman wrote about her desire to have descendants who are recognized as First Nations, 100 percent if possible, so that her community will have a population large enough to access certain rights.

This woman articulated her struggle from a gendered perspective, but also from the desire to stand as a First-Nations person before the state and keep her tribal land. Her anxieties over whom to date, a white man or a man with a certain blood quantum recognized by the Canadian state, revealed the dilemma produced by the state: how to accept its definition and then use that same categorization to dismantle the practices that strip First-Nations peoples of their territories. Upholding blood quantum can simultaneously be read as state oppression and as resistance. The political category of "Indigenous" and the ways it manifests has real, crucial consequences in seemingly private areas of life, such as the choice of whom to date.

I later read an article by Lisa Charleyboy, a woman from the Tsilhqot'in nation. She was writing about how, as a First-Nations woman in Canada, where marriage and dating are complicated issues, she was seeking a partner with at least 25 percent "Indigenous blood." Blood quantum made her feel vulnerable, and she started talking about this with other women. Fortunately, more and more people are questioning blood quantum and how it shapes the experiences of First-Nations women in Canada.

I was initially surprised to read these stories and to hear others by Native American women in the United States who define themselves based on their percentage of "native blood." My lived experience places me at a remove from these concerns, as I would never have thought about the implications of choosing a non-Indigenous or a mestizo partner (in the case of Mexico). Despite being an Indigenous woman like them, I did not share or know those concerns. This difference disturbed me greatly, and I realized something obvious, to which I somehow had not given importance in my own narratives: all Indigenous women belong to nations without a state—this is what groups us under the category of "Indigenous"—but each state determines how it wields that category and reinvents oppression. Many of our anxieties, desires, and reflections as Indigenous women, which all seem extremely personal, are responses and reactions to the specific ways in which each nation-state sanctions "being Indigenous." The structure will not be eroded by our refusal to identify as such, at least not as individuals.

LANGUAGE

These contrasting experiences made me realize that although I do not share the same concerns as First-Nations women in Canada, they left me with an open question: What are the state mechanisms here in Mexico that mediate the category "Indigenous" to which I am responding? The Mexican state has legally determined that self-identification is the only criterion needed for a person to be considered Indigenous; however, in practice, this matter works in a different way. For decades, the Mexican government has used linguistic criteria to establish Indigenous identity. While markers such as traditional dress were gradually diluted, largely by the Mexican state's mestizo-making enterprise, language has been used as a marker to count and record the number of Indigenous people in Mexico. Though the Indigenous population in Mexico exceeds the number of Indigenous language speakers, the National Institute of Statistics and Geography (INEGI) points to the use of language as a key factor in calculating how many Indigenous people reside in the country. Paradoxically, it has been the public policies of the Mexican state that have caused the accelerated loss of Indigenous languages.

These mechanisms directly impact the collective imagination of Indigenous peoples: not speaking the Indigenous language of one's community is often interpreted as a loss that renders Mixes, Zapotec, or Mixtec peoples half-Indigenous, if not mestizo. Here, blood quantum has been reconfigured as a language quantum. In this context, within the struggle of the Indigenous movement and official discourse alike, Indigenous women are often assigned the role of guardians responsible for the intergenerational transmission of Indigenous languages. This not only essentializes the role of women as linguistic guardians but also ignores the fact that colonialism and racism perpetuated against Indigenous peoples disrupt such transmission. Indigenous women have played a fundamental role in the transmission of Indigenous languages and traditional knowledge, and women's movements have in many cases engaged in linguistic resistance, but it is not our sole responsibility to maintain the vitality of Indigenous languages. The solution involves dismantling the racist structures that both halt the intergenerational transmission of Indigenous languages and eliminate the spaces where these languages are spoken.

The linguistic marker used by the Mexican state is reproduced in different practices and requirements of state bureaucracy, and even by well-meaning programs and allies. On one occasion, while interviewing for a graduate fellowship for Indigenous people, I was asked to speak Mixe to verify that I am indeed Indigenous. Having to speak in front of people who do not understand what you are saying but who can decide that it "sounds" like an Indigenous language made me feel vulnerable. I did not see it then, but my experience is in some ways tied to the vulnerability that First-Nations women in Canada feel when faced with questions of blood quantum: it is the vulnerability of having to meet and be defined by the markers used by the state to deem you Indigenous enough. I am not worried about whether the father of my hypothetical daughter is a

BLOOD, LANGUAGE, SURNAME   13

non-Indigenous person—he could be born in Tokyo; as long as my daughter speaks Mixe and is part of my community she will be considered Mixe and therefore Indigenous by the state. At the end of the day, my concerns stem from the idea that I am responsible for that transmission of language because I position myself in that struggle. I imagine that for Lisa Charleyboy, in Canada, the issue of language is less cause for worry than the search for a partner recognized as 100 percent First Nations.

SURNAME

In reading and talking to the K'iche' political scientist Gladys Tzul Tzul,[3] I learned of the vital role that Indigenous women in Totonicapán, Guatemala, play in defending communal ownership of their lands. Communal land ownership is fundamental to their resistance against the state, and it is the basis of what Tzul calls the reproduction of life. In order to defend their land from the ever-present threat of state appropriation, they maintain its communal status through a system that involves passing down a series of patrilineal surnames. In this way, kinship is used as a legal strategy for defending communal lands, since these surnames are officially recognized by the state. According to Tzul, one of the questions women ask themselves in this context is what happens to the children of women who decide to start a family with a man who does not bear one of the surnames that protect the communal ownership of the land, and what is the political status of women who do not decide to form a new family unit? Even if they do form a relationship

---

3. Gladys Tzul Tzul, *Sistemas de gobierno comunal indígena: mujeres y tramas de parentesco en Chuimeq'ena',* published in Guatemala (Sociedad Comunitaria de Estudios Estratégicos, 2016).

with a man who has one of the officially recognized surnames, these women will still be vulnerable precisely because of the doubly articulated position they are in—because of their gender and their resistance to the colonial order as Indigenous people defending their territory.

OPPRESSION AND RESISTANCE

For me, when it comes to my site of enunciation as an Indigenous woman, neither surname nor blood quantum represent sources of reflection or worry. However, for many First-Nations women in Canada and Indigenous women in Totonicapán, these are pressing issues to which they must respond and propose alternatives.

Our different concerns and responses demonstrate the power of the state in establishing "Indigenous" as a category. However, this statement seems dangerous to me, because although it is true that the state's recognition determines who is considered Indigenous and how Indigenous communities are viewed, it is also true that as Indigenous women in the struggle, we are not passive: the Indigenous communities to which we belong have turned the requirements imposed by the state into acts of resistance against the state itself.

The ambivalence of these responses leads to personal anxieties that are heightened by the intersection of the colonial and patriarchal systems that Aura Cumes discusses. The ever-creative responses to blood quantum, language, and official recognition of surnames are raised as forms of subversion to the oppression perpetuated by nation-states, which in every case also appeals to the relationship with the patriarchal system that impacts Indigenous women. While the mere fact of belonging to nations without a state unites us as Indigenous women,

BLOOD, LANGUAGE, SURNAME

the nation-states within which our nations are encapsulated dictate to us how to be "completely" or 100 percent Indigenous. Fortunately, our responses have the potential to become tools of resistance for our peoples. Fortunately, it is not the state that certifies what it is to be Tsilhqot'in, Mixe, or K'iche' women.

From these sites of enunciation, we call into question the narrative, often reproduced by Western feminism, that the gender oppression of Indigenous women has to do with Indigenous societies and not with "Indigenous" as a category. As Indigenous women in different nation-states such as Canada, Mexico, and Guatemala, we are always responding from complex positionalities shaped by different systems. These responses always have the potential to challenge the colonialist imposition of nation-states; an initial vulnerability is thus transformed into a subversive idea that challenges the category and the word "Indigenous" at its very root. And therein lies at least one of its powers.

Marina Azahua
tr. Julia Sanches

REBELLION OF THE CASSANDRAS

Then no longer will my prophecies peek
like some timid bride from behind a veil.
No: they will blow clear as a wind at
sunrise, they will surge like a wave against
the new light with a woe to eclipse its
shining. No more riddles. You will be
my witness, running alongside me as I
uncover crimes long past . . . I know the
legacy of crime within this house.

—Cassandra in Aeschylus's *The Oresteia*,
tr. A. Shapiro and P. Burian

The problem is that they don't
believe us.

—Mariana Enriquez,
"The Things We Lost in the Fire,"
tr. Megan McDowell

DECADES OF SAYING the same thing: they're killing us. And in return, silence. As if we alone could hear ourselves. As if we were crying out in some faraway place or in the middle of nowhere, miles from anything. Or maybe our cries were only heard—prey to the crucial distinction between hearing and listening. Did our words fail to breach the gulf between perception and incomprehension because we spoke them in a twisted language, with the wrong words, or in an inadequate tone? It's always our fault. Did they not want to listen, or could we not be listened to? If by some miracle our voices could be heard, did this mean they were also easy to ignore? Easy to ignore, perhaps, because it was easier not to believe us.

When we scream *they're killing us*, it isn't a plea. It isn't just a cry or complaint. When we say they're killing us, we're voicing a prophecy. A portent that carries the manifest destiny of its tenuous credibility. And nearly always seems fated to be seen as an exaggeration . . . until it comes true. Over and over and over again, it comes true. The central issue is pain and death. And after that, the anguish of our ever-so-fragile credibility: the harm that stems from the fact that the warning was given a long time before the prophecy is fulfilled—and we know it will be fulfilled, again—though it could have been avoided. The problem starts with our not being believed. Which leads to our being killable.

In Greek myth, Cassandra is the daughter of the last king of Troy. Birthed and nursed by Hecuba, she is the sister of the tortured corpse of Hector and the unwilling sister-in-law of Helen. Cassandra shouldered the burden of presaging the fall of Troy. But no one believed her. She augured the dangers of her brother Paris's abduction of Helen and the consequences of her arrival in Troy. But no one believed her. She foresaw the tragedy of accepting peace offerings—Trojan horses—from the enemy, but no one believed her. And Troy fell.

This is what I will tell the girls in my life who will inherit the future: I will them that for a period of time, which we could refer to as *forever*, we knew with near-absolute certainty that the future was the grief of waking up day after day with the news of *una más*, another woman assaulted or murdered. One pain after another. Every time, we warned them it would happen again. And over and over and over, the prophecy was fulfilled. A daily, aching testament to the peril of living in the world as a woman. After attesting to the curse and mourning each loss, the knowledge dropped back into the pits of our stomachs, in anticipation of another piece of bad news. Instinct, they called it. Gut feeling. I imagine the women of yore felt similarly when their babies died one after another in a world where infant mortality was unthinkably high by current standards. My great-grandmother gave birth sixteen times, and six of her children died. I imagine her harboring the panicked belief, after each baby's death, that the others were bound to die too. Don't get too attached, they said. In the twentieth century, the shadowy specter of infant mortality was subdued—to a point and in particular territories. Maybe time will also pass for our present-day fears. Hopefully, in the future, women will find it unimaginable that we spent every day awaiting news of yet another woman murdered, raped, battered, or harassed. The dream is that future women will find our experience unimaginable.

In many ways, growing up means discovering the suffering of the women around us. Every wound is a warning: It happened to me; careful it doesn't happen to you. It happened to her; careful it doesn't happen to you. Living means training yourself to respond to inevitable violence (in vain, since there's no way to control the finger on the trigger of aggression). In many ways, our lives are spent trying to evade that violence. It's exhausting work.

Cassandra learned to read the future in the house of the god Apollo. In one version of the myth, a serpent whispers lessons in her ear about becoming a prophet; in another version, the gift is from Apollo himself, who gives it to Cassandra in an attempt to seduce her. Whatever the source of the gift, Cassandra rejects Apollo. She makes a choice not to share her body with him. Furious, Apollo punishes Cassandra by forcing her to accept the gift of divination and then adding a curse: she would foresee the future, but no one would believe her.

Here are some other things I will tell the girls of the future about what it's like to live with this knowledge in your gut. First: it will rarely be believed. Second: nonetheless, we still know how to experience joy. Third: it will make you feel like nothing can be done. But there, in the stench and darkness of abuse, despite the endless waves of pain and blood, we find each other.

Cassandra was punished for saying no. For resisting the god's seduction. When did silence become the only form of resistance? When did our cry stop being heard? Who made silence a synonym of "no"?

I will tell the girls of the future that in the dawn of the twenty-first century, in the midst of an endless cycle of murder, rape, and infamy, there was a great meeting of Cassandras. One day these weary clairvoyants, whom no one believed, met in the center of their shared pain, heard each other's voices, and decided they had no choice but to believe in one another blindly—with all the risks this entails, all the imperfections of a procedure that exists outside the logic of *innocent until proven guilty*. But this time their rage was more powerful than the legacy of a rotten law.

On August 16, 2019, during a series of protests sparked by the news that six Mexico City police officers had raped a young woman, a large group of women gathered in the nation's capital and covered the monument to Independence on Paseo de la Reforma in graffiti. The statue of Winged Victory—not an

REBELLION OF THE CASSANDRAS 23

angel, actually—looms above the column at the center of the monument. Victory, eyes fixed on the horizon, could not see the women below. And even though Victory could not turn her gaze toward them, in her shadow an enraged outcry burst forth as paint.

In 1957, sixty-two years before the rebellion of the Cassandras, the Winged Victory toppled to the ground during a 7.8 magnitude earthquake, its shattered body strewn around the base of the monument where, to this day, a goddess presides over each corner: Peace, War, Law, and Justice. The head of Nike, the goddess of victory, rolled along the concrete, her dismembered body sprawled between Peace and War. The sculpture was restored, and the following year Winged Victory stood once again above the city. But Nike's first face was never restored. Still broken, it can be seen today at the entrance of the Historic Archives of Mexico City, on Calle de Chile.

According to urban legend, Nike's injured face, its Greco-Latin features sculpted by artist Enrique Alciati, was based on the daughter of Antonio Rivas Mercado, beloved architect of General Porfirio Díaz, who commissioned the monument to Independence. Some fables claim the face belongs to his eldest daughter, Alicia; others say it is the face of his second daughter, Antonieta, though the time frame makes this second claim hard to believe. In yet another related or superimposed myth, Alicia is the young woman whose profile graces the medallion on the door that leads inside the column, where a mausoleum holds the remains of our nation's heroes.

Alicia is known for being Antonio's daughter and Antonieta's sister. And Antonieta is known primarily for being the lover of José Vasconcelos, a relationship that contributed to her death by suicide in Paris inside Notre-Dame in 1931. Heartbreak, they say. A gunshot to the chest. A gun that belonged to Vasconcelos himself. Apparently, it was a nightmare to have to reconsecrate the cathedral in the wake of such a sin. But long before Vasconcelos broke her heart, Antonieta was a writer, an intellectual, a feminist, and a patron of the arts. A key player in early twentieth-century Mexican culture. Needless to say, she is predominantly remembered for her physical image and for the terminal pain inflicted on her by a man.

Eighty-eight years after Antonieta's death, a group of enraged women sprayed a mix of purple, green, pink, black, and red paint on the base of the monument her father had built. The white marble was stained, the metal marked, and the hindquarters of the bronze lion, placidly shepherded by a winged cherubin, tattooed in neon pink with the sign of Venus: ♀

Green bandanas, pink glitter, and coils of purple smoke.

I'm not the best at defining or differentiating between a protest, a march, a demonstration, and a riot. But I know when I see a revolt. The intervention on the monument to Independence was not, strictly speaking, part of a demonstration; it wasn't a protest with a manifesto or a list of demands. Screaming furiously because they are murdering us is not a demand. It was a revolt. A surge of rage that needed to be let out.

The girls of the future ought to grow up knowing that the women of their past reached the tipping point over a festering wound. One day, sick and tired, those Cassandras rebelled. They faced fears racked up over centuries, embedded in their skin, lodged in their memories, and focused all their hopes on becoming difficult bodies deployed time and again in public spaces, in ways never before thought possible.

On August 16, the monument to Independence became the reverse of an oracle, naming the past that was also the present and which the Cassandras had long considered an inevitable future: a femicide state. The monument's marble plaque, above the lion and cherubin, now bears graffiti that reads: *México Feminicida*. Beneath it, the plaque's text reads, in Roman type: *From the nation to the heroes of our independence*. A dedication.

Who is the nation? Who are the heroes? Who makes up a country that has become femicidal? The state is a macho rapist, declared the performance *A Rapist in Your Path* by the Chilean collective Las Tesis, and hundreds of women sang with pleasure (*It wasn't my fault, not where I went or what I was wearing*) and recrimination (*You are the rapist*) outside the Presidential Palace. A few weeks later, during marches set off by the femicide of Ingrid Escamilla, they set fire to the front door of that same palace.

A minor archive of messages painted on the monument to Independence:

> The fatherland is a murderer
> Femicide = national heritage
> Self-defense now
> Alive, I want you alive
> Ni una más
> Justice
> It won't fall, we'll knock it down
> We won't be toyed with
> No + fear
> Cops rape
> Rapists
> They don't protect me they rape me
> Rapist cops
> Pigs rape
> Rapist
> Rapist pigs
> Rapigs
> Femicide fatherland
> State crime
> Murderous nation
> Abort the patriarchy
> Rapists' members go in blenders
> Mexico femicide nation
> All women are oppressed
> Death to machos
> Never again
> Ni una menos
> Yes to life
> There is no trade without johns

Sick and tired
We're not scared anymore
Fight like a ♀
Silence = violence
For the ones who never came home
You will not have the comfort of our silence

A woman added two question marks to either side of the inscription at the base of the statue representing Peace. The text now reads: ¿PAZ?

Around the frame of the door to the mausoleum, a series of pink hands glow in neon. The imprints of the fingers and palms of women who are sick and tired. Traces of the temporary appropriation of this monument; vestiges fashioned out of rebellious bodies; a gestural testimony like the handprint signatures in cave paintings. We were here, they say.

In the wake of the riots sparked by the rebellion of the Cassandras, news channels were flooded with outraged voices denouncing the desecration of their national patrimony. We responded by taking to the streets and shouting that we wished we were walls, so people would be as outraged when we are wounded . . . The more conservative voices were sure that the guardians of our patrimony and the protectors of our monuments would be the most outraged of all. But in response, a collective of conservators called Restauradoras con Glitter made their position on the graffiti public. Armed with their expertise, they called for the writing not to be removed and demanded a detailed record of the messages on the monument, citing their historic importance and symbolic power. An excerpt of their open letter makes note of the inscriptions and says, "Their preservation should serve as a concrete reminder of the shameful violence in our country, and they should under no circumstance be removed until the gender-based violence that assails our nation has been dealt with. . . . A team of professionals should be appointed to meticulously document these graffiti, which are of social, historical, and symbolic importance, in order to preserve our collective memory of this event and its causes."

Sometimes we forget the details because in the moment they seem obvious; as time passes, they fade. They are fleeting, and so we need to hold on to them: the call-to-action messages before the demonstration urged people to bring purple glitter and dress in black. Demonstration after demonstration, the collective Marabunta safeguarded the protestors by standing between them and the police. Purple smoke became a twin symbol of the raised fist. No one really knows how August 16 went from being a peaceful march to a protest that deployed direct action. From then on, that day's unbridled rage would be felt at every march sparked by another act of violence. Terrified, the government would spend the next few months protecting hero-shaped hunks of stone and shielding monuments in plastic wrap and plywood boards.

But not all of the graffitied monuments harbored heroes. On that day in August, on their way to the monument, protestors directed their rage at a police precinct on Calle de Florencia.

REBELLION OF THE CASSANDRAS 29

Scrawling the word *rapists* on the façade of a precinct is a necessary act in a country where officers were ordered, in 2006, to sexually torture detained women in Atenco. This rage is necessary in a country where the majority of women detained by the police are subjected to sexual violence. This rage is necessary in a country where it is perfectly feasible for a group of police officers to rape an underage girl on her way home.

Months later, in November 2019, on International Day for the Elimination of Violence Against Women, the Benito Juárez Hemicycle was submitted to an intervention. In February 2020, it was the headquarters of sensationalist newspaper *La Prensa*, for publishing explicit front-page photographs of the mutilated body of Ingrid Escamilla, who was murdered by her partner. Finally, before the pandemic curbed the momentum of these revolts, bringing the whole world to a stop, a monumental demonstration on March 8, 2020, in honor of International Women's Day, was followed by a massive strike where women withdrew from the streets. The walkout was reminiscent of Aristophanes's *Lysistrata*, a play in which women go on strike (boycotting sex in that instance) to stop a war. In this case, the absence of women from the streets, work, and public spaces aimed to draw attention to what would happen if we all disappeared, while also seeking to end a war: the war against us.

If we were to make a list of all the messages scrawled on monuments and buildings during the rebellion of the Cassandras, we would find that these graffiti were, above all, a verdict. In contrast, the messages handwritten on signs were primarily for us—internal reflections, meditations for friends and strangers:

messages for witnesses. The graffiti on monuments and buildings, public transit stops, walls, and statues, were by and large accusatory. Graffiti as a tool for bringing down a monument without needing to topple it.

What is a monument?

Because we know. Because we have always known. Because we are sick and tired of this knowledge and of our recurring pain. Sick and tired of not being listened to. Sick and tired of being pegged as crazy, over and over and over again ... Finally, we realized that if the law won't listen, we can at least listen to each other.

Cassandra was raped at the foot of a monument. Cassandra was ignored and taken for a madwoman and locked in a tower. I wonder if she prophesied her own rape, or if that event was indistinguishable from all the other omens. The rape of a seer at the foot of the statue of Athena, the goddess of wisdom, perfectly illustrates how, even when we can read the future, there are times when our own futures are illegible. We tend to believe violence happens to other women, and yet when we are trapped in our own horror stories, we can't open our mouths to speak them.

We know. We always know. Because there are warnings. Sometimes we stay quiet, others we sound the alarm. Still, it happens again. We know it's going to happen. We know he's going to hit her. We know he's going to kill her . . . and there's nothing we can do to stop it. I think about the time she called me to say she was leaving and taking the kids, that she had packed their things in garbage bags and hidden them in trash cans outside the house, and that she would leave while he was on his night shift. I think about the moment she realized her husband was drugging her . . . for goodness knows how long. I think about how, for a long time, while she was being drugged, many of us thought she was unstable, crazy. I think about all the years we sensed—what's the difference between sensing and knowing?—that he was dangerous, that he was capable of hurting her, that he was already hurting her, even though it seemed impossible for her to leave. I think about another she who avoided murder by escaping to the neighbor's house. And another she whose partner was psychologically abusive and publicly humiliated her year after year. I think about a high-school classmate who didn't come over one Saturday our senior year to complete a group assignment and was found dead that evening in a nearby park. I think about the feeling I've had for decades that she could have been someone else, any of us. And I think about how that feeling has become run-of-the-mill, almost second nature. I think about the time I was saved by a split-second decision, but others weren't. I think about how, even though they didn't escape violence, they lived. And I celebrate them alive. And I think about the unassailable courage of their continued existence, and how their radiant happiness is the best revenge.

During the siege of Troy, Ajax the Lesser raped Cassandra while she was seeking refuge at the altar of Athena's temple. She was brutalized inside the safe haven of the goddess of wisdom, who is also a virgin goddess because it seems women can only have wisdom if they are virgins, madwomen, or witches; when virgins, they are goddesses and when witches or madwomen, they are exiled. This transgression was not without consequence. The rape of Cassandra sparked the goddess's radiant fury. Athena asked Poseidon to help her get revenge, which is how practically the entire Greek fleet was shipwrecked in a disastrous storm on its victorious journey home. If the cornerstone of *The Iliad* is Helen's abduction, then *The Odyssey* would not exist without Cassandra's rape.

Being a woman means growing up with the certainty that our bodies always already harbor the condition of possibility of potentially experiencing danger. Being a woman means getting used to this state of affairs. And sometimes, being a woman means getting tired of getting used to it. We know they can kill us, rape us, beat us, abuse us. . . . We've adapted to this reality and done our best not to expose ourselves. I can still remember the look of terror on my mother's face the day she realized her daughters—not yet five years old—were already potential victims of sexual violence. I remember my certainty as a child that I shouldn't trust men.

The year 2019 ended appropriately with the Second International Encounter of Women in Struggle, which took place in December in Zapatista territory. Hundreds of women said they never felt as safe as they did during those few days when their territory was populated exclusively by women.

REBELLION OF THE CASSANDRAS 33

I think about the woman I helped move so she could get away from her violent husband. Among her possessions I found an object symptomatic of our day and age: a printed violence meter, a tool to identify levels of abuse. At what point did we start assigning units of measure to the forms of violence perpetrated against women? Yellow: he screams at you. Orange: he beats you. Red: he kills you. At which of these warm shades do you decide to run for your life? It seems impossible to tell; sometimes there is no warning prior to the wave of pain that crashes over our bodies. When we know that we live in a permanent state of vulnerability, what does it mean to know? How can we plan accordingly?

Is it possible to build a monument to our pain? Maybe an elusive one, a portable monument that's hard to define: a network of affections erected around our vulnerability. What sustains us when the material scaffolding of the home that shelters us is lost? The house, the body—lost, trespassed, broken. Friendship, mutual care, and sisterhood step up to buttress the pain. But what are the threads holding this strength? Sometimes I wonder if we're ready to help each other heal all the wounds we've had to open to take up this fight. I think about the anti-monument outside the Palacio de Bellas Artes, the sculpture that ceases to be a monument and becomes something else, built by women to honor those of us who did not come home.

How to write a retrospective of that sea change? You could say 2019 was a pivotal year to be a woman in Mexico. Writing about that year is a collective undertaking that remains incomplete. From the #MeToo movement that exploded in April 2019 and the 2020 International Women's Day march, to the collective struggle of the mothers of victims of femicide and disappearance and the struggle for sexual and reproductive rights, women's struggles—both inclusive and overflowing, with their various nuances—are like countless birds released into the air. Some call it the fourth wave of feminism. Others call it women's struggle. I'm partial to the latter because framing it this way doesn't pin it to a specific historical moment; even though 2019 was doubtless a crucial year and it's important to write the story as it happened, it was also part of a larger tide that has been surging for years, from untold depths that cannot be fully gleaned in the present.

The deepest source of our rage is that we are sick and tired of the fact that no matter how much we struggle, how much we fight, how much we scream . . . women are going to keep being murdered, beaten, and raped. We will always have to fight on two fronts: on one front, we fight for the memory of the women we have lost, for justice and reparations, and against impunity; on the other front, we wage unceasing battle to end all this death. Will our struggle ever put an end to all this death?

How do we put an end to these deaths? Could Cassandra have prevented the fall of Troy with only her knowledge of what the horse contained?

I read pencil markings in the margins of a library book. I sense the previous reader was a woman. I'm not sure why; I just know. The first page of the book is cluttered with fragments, ideas, quotes, excerpts, page references. On the top left: "The desire for truth is stronger than death." In a circle, a hand once wrote: "The madwoman: the end of the torture of pretension. Madness: a trait associated with women." In the bottom corner: "Women associated with madness: Ophelia, Lady Macbeth, etc." Practically in the fold of the page: "Madness is a safety mechanism used by women to speak the truth." The word *truth* is underlined. The annotated book is Christa Wolf's *Cassandra*.

Is a gut feeling madness? Where do we speak from? Historically, it seems women have always had to speak from madness, lack of reason, and excess in order to be heard. We've had to become unreasonable. No riddles anymore, Cassandra said. I know the legacies of crime within this house. Nuances undermine, which is why we choose not to topple monuments but instead scrawl on them our words, unreasonably. This is how our truths landed, finally, at the feet of their petrified monuments.

Gestures, sounds: that other monument. A monument that doesn't live in the written word. This is not its archive. That monument lives in all the videos and voice messages sent from the march. The wailing of women, for example. The first time I heard that sound was in a prison scene in *The Battle of Algiers*, when political prisoners howled in protest like grieving owls while their colleague was led to his execution. *Zaghareet*, is how they refer to that cry. How to onomatopoeically render that wail, which is almost like birdsong, an expression of sorrow and celebration? How to render that war cry when a hundred mouths are emitting it at the same time?

We are in grief, in grief, aggrieved, aggrieved, aggrieved, grieved in grieving, bereaved, bereaved, grieving, grieving, grieving, grieving, grieving, grieving, grieving, grieving, grieving in grief, grief.

"I'm sick of it I'm sick of it sick sick sick sick sick sick sick sick sick sick sick sick sick sick sick sick sick sick sick sick sick sick sick sick sick sick sick sick sick sick sick sick sick sick sick sick sick sick sick sick sick sick sick sick sick sick sick sick sick sick sick sick sick sick sick sick sick sick sick sick sick sick sick sick sick sick sick sick sick sick sick sick sick sick sick sick sick sick sick sick sick," wrote Simone de Beauvoir in her short story "Monologue." Reading the piece as a teenager left an impression on me. Her outburst of sincerity taught me about the power of voice. "Monologue" is the third of three stories in *The Woman Destroyed*, where de Beauvoir also writes, "All women think they are different; they all think there are some things that will never happen to them; and they are all wrong." Flaubert is cited in the epigraph to the piece, which reads, "The monologue is her form of revenge."

I can still remember how dizzy that incessant repetition made me feel: sick sick sick. . . . Reading those words, I felt as if my darkness were part of a lineage. The sensation caused by the repetition in "Monologue" is similar to the feeling I had when I found out my friend's mother has a habit of going to Los Dinamos forest to scream in solitude, whenever she is overwhelmed by grief about life. The image of a woman screaming surrounded by trees, where no one can hear her—but she screams just the same—is as devastating to me as it is comforting. Part of me thinks it might be an omen resigned to having no interlocutor, but that must be spoken, nonetheless. Where can we scream that we are sick and tired if there is no forest? We will need to plant new trees among which to howl out our sorrows. I hope that in the future we won't need forests to run to so we can scream that we are sick and tired. . . . Has that moment come? No. We live in a world where the president still goes on television and tells people that 90 percent of reported incidents of violence against women are false.

Are we there yet? Will it be much longer? The girls of today— the women of the future—ask anxiously: Are we there yet? As we await a future when our cries are no longer stuck in our throats and our prophecies caught in our guts, a future when we can talk about our rebellion the same way we talk about suffragettes, we are still faced with the arduous task of surveying the damages.

On the morning of March 8, 2020, hours before the monumental demonstration honoring International Women's Day, the Zócalo started filling with names. The names of scores of women murdered in Mexico since 2016 were painted on the ground around the flagpole. This is how the day began, with some women prepping the city's main square for the arrival of other women on foot: mothers, sisters, daughters, cousins, friends. There is a permanent metal circle on one side of the flagpole, the ghost of the first column of the monument to independence they had attempted to build there. Now, on top of that circle, the foundation of the column that was never built, lies the ghost of another timeless, ephemeral monument: a white-painted stroke of the names of 3,200 women who never returned home. As many names as possible were painted—after nightfall, after the march ended and women were done dancing around a bonfire, after candles were lit and words spoken, after a black flag was raised in lieu of the nation's—before a government clean-up crew washed away the legitimate monumentality of those names with the perfect efficiency of a state that does not know how to listen.

Their names on the surface of the city's central plaza. The trace of their presence after they were erased.

The palimpsest of signs on our country's monuments is vast. Were they visible, the layers of letters would be thick. In the final days of February 2015, overcome by a different kind of pain—about the forced disappearance of forty-three students from Ayotzinapa—a group of protestors also graffitied the monument to Independence. A journalist covering the clean-up included the reflections of an architect who happened to walk by in his story. While Mexico City's clean-up crew used solvents and steel wool to arduously erase the words "justice will come when . . ." from between the stones, the circumstantial expert explained that instead of cleaning the monument, the solvents were damaging it, because "they were opening its pores and forcing the ink inside. Meaning, they aren't actually removing the graffiti so much as pushing it deeper. All the pigment is migrating inward." Decades of spray-paint revolts later, how many messages are embedded in the matter of our national monuments? I hope the monuments contain every trace of our pain and become an intimate archive of every message inked on their surfaces. If the graffiti embodies how sick and tired we are, may it migrate to the heart of every monument so that the fulfilled prophecy of our rage may never be erased.

Fernanda Latani M. Bravo
tr. Gabriela Ramirez-Chavez

**HEARTQUAKES:
AN EMOTIONAL GEOGRAPHY**

WE KNOW THAT the adult heart beats between seventy and one hundred times per minute. But there are moments in life when a woman's heart doesn't beat, it quakes, trembles—vascular-tectonic movements caused by fractures and pain. Pain that, as César Vallejo writes, "opens trenches in the toughest faces and the strongest backs." In this exploration of emotional geography, I want to tell you about those heartquakes and their aftershocks in a woman, a woman of flesh and bone—sometimes more bone, other times more flesh, sometimes earth, sometimes dust.

The mother of all tectonic plates, the Pacific Plate, unleashed her power on her daughters the Cocos and Caribbean Plates on the night of September 7, 2017 (a date we Zapotecs will never forget). My mother spoke to me with that same power from her hammock in the hallway, two months after the 8.2 magnitude earthquake devastated a large part of the Isthmus of Tehuantepec in Southern Oaxaca, along with my most intimate territory, my body, though I did not realize it at the time.

In my childhood and teenage years, I often questioned why I had so many profound, seemingly irreconcilable differences with my mother, Leonor Soledad. If we were so similar and so close, if I was the girl my mother had longed for—and had in fact "fervently prayed for"—why did we have to ignore and avoid each other to live together like two cockroaches in a crack? Maybe it is due in part to my mother's name. A name conjures a thing, and my mother's name, which means loneliness or solitude, suggests her hermetic, complex being, which she and I had not yet overcome.

You may be wondering: What is the connection between the 2017 earthquake and the constant tension I have with my mother? Both events have caused me pain and inspired me to rebuild myself from the ruins of the person I had been.

I want to begin by mapping my childhood experience. I was raised in a family of four men—three brothers and my father, a mountain walker—and my mother, heir to the rhythms, tastes, and smells of "the green Antequera," Oaxaca City. My childhood involved moving around a lot and adapting. I traveled valleys, mountains, and hills; I saw pine and oak trees, cloud forests, deciduous and evergreen forests; I touched my first thick mosses and grasslands, I tasted pineapples, pears, loquats, coconuts, and guavas. Still, the traditional distribution of roles within my family led to physical distance from my father, who worked outside our home, and a growing tension with the woman who loves me most but who had to care for four children under unfavorable conditions: two teenagers, Diego and Juan, and two infants, Ernesto and Fernanda.

I was fifteen or sixteen when I took a biography of Salvador Allende (by a Russian writer) from my father Rey David's bookcase. I was intrigued because the first photo in the book is of Fidel Castro and Allende. I recognized Fidel from other photos and because the Cuban Revolution, socialism, and the liberation of the Americas were things Rey David, my brothers, and my mother discussed over dinner, although my mother weighed in very little, saying these were not her preferred topics of conversation. Dad studied sociology at the

National Autonomous University of Mexico (UNAM) and was the only one of eight children that my grandparents, Juana Ordáz Cortés and Ignacio Meléndez, put through college. It was precisely during the seventies and eighties that my father found his way to Marxist critical thought due to his activism in the Coalition of Workers, Farmers, and Students of the Isthmus (COCEI) and at college. We grew up hearing about my father's college days, how my grandmother Juana would pack him dried shrimp with totopos, but he'd sell them to his friends and professors, pinching off the shrimp heads.

The Salvador Allende biography is from that time. It was my introduction to socialist readings and to a history I could hardly believe; between Neruda's poems, Victor Jara's songs, and excerpts from speeches, I learned about Allende's life and made the ideas my father repeated at home my own. A rebellious critical thinker was born then, one who wanted to travel to Cuba with her father. That young leftist activist who I used to be, who admired everything about her father, made me the woman I am today. Without a doubt, this education and my grandmother Juana's work as an embroiderer and rezadora, whose prayers had the power to heal, strengthened my identity as a Zapotec woman who, like many women whose umbilical cords root them in the Isthmus of Tehuantepec, toil under the sun and the extreme heat to support their families.

WHEN I WAS eight years old, we moved for our father's job to Ixtlán de Juárez, in the famous Sierra Juárez or northern Sierra of Oaxaca. There, the cold climate, the culture and way of life, as well as maternal and household responsibilities led to the first clashes between my mother and me. During this time, I came into my own as an extroverted, rebellious, and defiant girl. That is how I describe myself now, but back then my mother would say, "Tani, quit whining and talking back." That behavior earned me, until a couple of years ago, her strong disapproval and harsh punishments. Soledad didn't know she was suffering from what is known as repetition compulsion: she had been disciplined as a child for "talking back," and now she was doing the same to me. Along with these first fights, I began to notice the profound misery my mother felt at the time, because living in a place that was not her own plunged her into a deep sadness. She tells me that she stopped weaving, dancing, and reading in order to raise and support our family.

This childhood lies at the core of my being. I have carried it throughout the difficult moments in my life, among them the earthquake on September 7. That night, minutes before 11:49 p.m., when the devastating earthquake hit, I closed my eyes and thought about my mother. I had not seen her in seven days. I lay down to sleep and began to reflect on my new life as an educator, how hard this period had been for me, transitioning from being a student and feminist activist in the streets to the formality of being a teacher. The deep blow it had dealt to my nomadic lifestyle, my freedoms, and my anarchist worldview.

A few minutes later, I felt my bed move. The earth rocked back and forth in a motion I knew perfectly well, like the rocking of a hammock. I went out to the communal courtyard and heard the deep rumble of the earth's crust. That was when I saw Magda, whom I now call the light-woman because she brought light into our night of anguish. Our eyes met, drawing us into each other's arms as the slow swaying of the earth turned into more than five minutes of violent shaking. Her words and my screams under the moonlight wove our fears together. Her daughter and my mother were the first things that crossed our minds when the tectonic phenomenon ended.

The next day, I traveled to meet my mother at our home in

Ixtepec. I arrived with my eyes full of dust from all the collapsed houses I had passed in Juchitán, Espinal, and Ixtaltepec. I'd had no food or water, the only thing that could revive me was arriving home to see her and my father. But they weren't there. I didn't know if they were okay, but inside the house everything seemed under control except for some cracks, fallen tiles, and broken glass. I realized that we were lucky our home had not been destroyed.

That same Friday afternoon, seeing my mother and knowing she was alive was enough for me to say that we were all right, because sometimes flesh, bones, and voices outweigh the soul, the body, and love.

On this feminist journey of reaffirming my love between women and for women, I felt that I needed to do something to support the rebuilding of people's hearts in my community and my region, which had been gravely affected by the huge earthquake. I remember well how a tweet I posted reached many people from other virtual spaces, stressing the dire need to help the Isthmian population as soon as possible, since the mainstream media was hardly covering the tragedy.

On September 11, Nanaxhi and Azalea—friends who became my sisters—and I decided to start collecting funds and food for areas that were almost impossible to reach. There was a sense of fear, uncertainty, and sadness because nobody knew what was going on. It was more than a seismic movement, and our grandmothers and mothers asked again and again: Why are these quakes happening? Why does the earth keep moving? Why us? I watched as Nanaxhi, the most affectionate of us three, reached out to offer a comforting hug. Seeing her head rest on another woman's, I imagined my mother and me offering each other love and comfort after the earthquake. I longed for that scene and wanted it to happen, but since I always arrived home at night, it never did. By that time, my mother was already half-asleep in her hammock in the hallway, and when she heard me come in, she'd only say, "Oh good, Tani, you're home. Rest well, daughter." I would fall asleep feeling a huge weight on my shoulders. Later, I realized that some of the weight I felt was the sadness of the people who had lost their homes.

The collection effort lasted for several days, as did the emotional barrier between me and my mother. Our labor was communal—gathering donations with Nanaxhi, Azalea, and my sister-in-territory Magaly in the rain and among the rubble, helping the women of BIBANI: Rebuilding with Identity to restore housing, or working with the feminist sisters of Nosotras en el Istmo—but my body was present almost everywhere I saw an urgent need. Pain entered my body through my eyes because of what I was seeing; it moved down to my stomach through my throat, which often hurt from skipping meals, getting soaked in the rain, and not talking about what I was experiencing. My nervous system was shot. I was often agitated; I cried little but grieved a lot; I had heart palpitations, and my lower back hurt so much. It was all taking a toll.

Those days were difficult for everyone, but I didn't dare admit that they were also difficult for me. My body, my territory, gave me the first warning when pain entered through the front door. My face was covered in acne, my hair—which I love because it connects me at the root to my grandmother Juana Cortés—was falling out: it was brittle, rough, and dry, that's the best way to describe it. My back felt the immense weight of other people's pain, to the point that I couldn't bend over or sleep in a hammock. I held stress in my shoulders, and anxiety was weaving a spiderweb of tension under my scalp. The second warning was that I stopped menstruating; I didn't bleed one month, and then another. Despite all this, I didn't dare listen to my body, which was clearly crying for help.

One morning, after several days of not being able to see my then-partner, I knew something was wrong—my Zapotec intuition told me so, and it was right. As if the pain in my body and soul were not enough, the tremors in my heart began: I discovered that my partner had cheated on me and had been avoiding me for days. I felt like an aftershock was splitting my heart.

But not even all this pain could move me to hug Soledad. I knew I would collapse if I took her hand and put my head in her lap, so I chose to live through my own earthquake and its aftershocks in secret, in the most private corners of my home. I rarely talked about this with my friends, and as a feminist, this really made me question how we've been taught to live through disappointment and betrayal. I hid my pain perfectly, and although my mother searched for me with her gaze, I kept to myself.

My relationship with my mother began to fracture, and everything we had been through in the aftermath of the earthquake, along with our refusal to hug each other and cry, made me realize we had all been affected differently. She and I each had to face certain things in order to heal. But I also knew I had inherited feelings and sorrows from her that weighed on me. My mother grew up without a father figure. When my grandmother was pregnant with my mother, my grandfather Jóse was murdered for defending a woman who, like him, was from the coast of Jamiltepec, Oaxaca. My grandmother Guadalupe carried that immense pain and perhaps passed it on to my mother through the umbilical cord. For many years, my mother lived with a profound melancholy, but she eventually decided to take a big step to save herself: she sought professional help. The pain that fell upon her body was the grief her mother had poured over her; my mother was willing to abort it, and so she did.

Those confrontations with my mother, all that sadness, the earthquake, and the work to rebuild the hearts of those affected by the earthquake, made me realize I needed to heal my relationship with my mother. But how? I began by recognizing that our mothers are our first models of strength, something all women know deep down, and that it wasn't too late. A ray of sunlight can sprout a seed even in the hardest ground.

I had to start by acknowledging those periods of hostility we've had since my childhood, puberty, and adolescence, which I no longer wanted to carry in my adulthood. Daring to heal the relationship with my mother, to become women who could live in harmony, was part of my constant process of identifying as a feminist, because I could not continue idealizing the harmonious relationships I cultivated with sisters or other feminists, while in my private life, my relationship with my mother was constantly erupting. As my mother says, "You can't be a light in the street but spread darkness at home."

In December 2018, I decided to go alone on a trip that would take me over four thousand miles away. My identity as a traveler guided me, and I gathered strength from the two halves of my heart. As I crossed natural borders, I knew that I had to follow through with the commitment my mother and I had made months earlier, sitting face to face. The great mountains of the Andes had granted me a space within their rocky being, and I knew it was the right moment to reunite with my past self, to hug myself and offer myself love and forgiveness for abandoning myself, and to move on. In the same way, I went on to imagine Leonor Soledad distraught, dejected, and furious in order to hug her and offer her love, so we could forgive each other for abandoning one another and begin the process of healing together. I finally realized that the same river runs through our stories, our pain, our grief, our rage, spilling out furiously into the ocean.

So many questions arose that I didn't know how to answer. Nonetheless, I began to see my mother not as a sorrowful woman but as a woman historically weighed down by the dynamics of invisibility—we need to fight for the freedom to name what happens to us. My mother had been surviving inherited sorrows that had overwhelmed her for many years, but which one day she decided to expel. In the same way, I now needed to follow through with the promise I had made to myself. I realized that to deny part of the personality traits we inherit from our mothers is also to deny our own history, and that the often-seismic relationship we have with our mothers must be redirected. Just like magma is expelled from inside the volcano, then flows as lava, becomes igneous rock upon contact with the air, and its ashes nourish the soil, my mother and I needed to expel our pain and become fertile ground for new blooms.

After I returned, almost six months passed before I felt my body, mind, and soul were strong enough for me to talk to my mother, to tell her about my trip, my journey through Wallmapu, my plans for the future, my reflections, and how the ancient mountains had embraced me. I was not the same woman after that fateful day engraved in the memory of my people, but I had the same love for Soledad. Now, I understood her better because I understood myself better. I had every intention of talking to her, but I hadn't found the right moment. I planned it many times, but that conversation never happened, so chance came to my rescue. A misunderstanding triggered a heated argument between us that escalated into a painful confrontation in the car. My father tried to calm the waters, wanting to mediate, but I told him it wasn't his battle or the place to share his opinion.

The earthquake was over, now it was time for us to build a new relationship from the rubble and tears. The Isthmus had already begun its rebirth, now it was our turn. Soledad was no longer alone and Latani had to reclaim her joy and honor the meaning of her name. It has been a few years since our heartquakes, and although we have not fully healed, we make progress every day because we have come to understand that it takes a long time to recover from a major seismic shift. We still need more time to pass but, as we wait, we love each other every day.

Dahlia de la Cerda
tr. Julianna Neuhouser

FEMINISM WITHOUT A
ROOM OF ONE'S OWN

I lack imagination you say.
No. I lack language.
The language to clarify
my resistance to the literate.
Words are a war to me.
They threaten my family.
To gain the word to describe the loss,
I risk losing everything.

> —Cherríe Moraga, "It's the Poverty"

The white fathers told us, I think, therefore I am;
and the Black mother in each of us—the poet—
whispers in our dreams, I feel therefore I can be free.

> —Audre Lorde, "Poetry is Not a Luxury"

INTRODUCTION

I write for the women who don't have a room of their own. For the women who write with babies on their tits and the women who don't write because they have babies on their tits. For the women who theorize while washing the dishes. For the women who theorize while washing clothes, while selling tamales in a rough neighborhood, because reflecting on the injustice of our economic model while selling de chile y de verde is also theorization. I write for the women who perrean sucio y hasta abajo. I write for the women who rhyme in their mother tongue, protesting the imposition of Spanish. I write for the women who don't read white men who want to explain the world without getting their shoes dirty. I am writing for the women who have abortions while working twelve-hour shifts in a shoe store. For the women who have abortions behind the backs of the state and their Christian fathers and their pro-life husbands.

I write for the women who say haiga. I write for the women who add nos to every verb. Íbanos and veníanos. I am writing, more than anything else, for the women who refuse to speak or write Spanish the way the Royal Academy of the Language dictates.

I write for the women who don't have a room of their own. For the women with a pad and a pen on the kitchen table because brilliant ideas come to them as they grind salsa in a molcajete. I write for the women who misspell and for the women who learned to rhyme by listening to street rap. For the women who have forgotten about having a room of their own because they have to work to support their children and their parents and life itself. I am writing for the women for whom writing is a fourth or fifth shift, pero se la rifan because words are a political act, the political act of the dispossessed.

I wrote this text without a room of my own. I wrote it in the dead time of my office job and while doing the laundry. I wrote it in my kitchen and on the steps down to the patio. I wrote it on the toilet and I wrote it as tears ran down my face and I wrote it because my psychiatrist told me that hitting people wasn't a good way of expressing my rage. I wrote it at my stall at the tianguis where I spent years selling used clothes in order to make it to the end of the month. I also wrote it on the Number 2 bus on my way to the mental hospital.

If this essay had a smell, it would smell like soap and disinfectant. If it had a taste, it would taste like tomatoes and onions and chiles de árbol and grilled nopal. If it had a sound, it would sound like the chaca-chaca-chaca of the washing machine with Los Acosta playing in the background. I wrote it without a room of my own and between paragraphs I gave myself breaks to dance to Wisin y Yandel. To Ivy Queen and Tego Calderón. This isn't anecdotal. It's political.

FOR THOSE EMERGING FROM THEIR ZULOS

In 2015, I met Itziar Ziga. Itziar was my favorite feminist writer at the time. Her book *Becoming Bitch* changed my position on feminism. I told her. As she signed my copy of *A Zulo of One's Own*, I told her that *Becoming Bitch* was the book that

FEMINISM WITHOUT A ROOM OF ONE'S OWN 57

led me to identify as a feminist. She got up and hugged me. It was very moving. Then came the epiphany. She signed my copy with the phrase, "For those emerging from their zulos."

Virginia Woolf said that *a room of one's own* is needed if a woman is to write, a space that means independence and autonomy. Ever since Woolf's day, the room of one's own has been a recurring thread in the fabric of feminist theorization. The room of one's own is an object of desire, the aspiration of any writer committed to the cause. The room of one's own is the goal because it not only means that you can write, but also that you managed to emancipate yourself enough to find somewhere to write. The room of one's own is the place where one writes. It's time. It's money. These are class, racial, and epistemic privileges. Not to mention the general consensus that any woman writer who wants her work to be fruitful should get herself one.

The room of one's own went unquestioned until the Chicana writer Gloria Anzaldúa came along and dotted the i's:

> Forget the room of one's own—write in the kitchen, lock yourself up in the bathroom. Write on the bus or the welfare line, on the job or during meals, between sleeping or waking. I write while sitting on the john. No long stretches at the typewriter unless you're wealthy or have a patron—you may not even own a typewriter. While you wash the floor or clothes listen to the words chanting in your body. When you're depressed, angry, hurt, when compassion and love possess you. When you cannot help but write.

A zulo, according to Wikipedia, is a hole or hiding place or clandestine location. A zulo is something that's not a room of one's own. A room of one's own isn't necessarily a physical space exclusively set aside for a woman to write; it can also be the privileges that allow a woman to write. Working less than eight hours a day is a room of one's own. Money and time to go to a café is a room of one's own. Silence at home is a room of one's own. A table and a computer is a room of one's own. Not sharing your home with ten people is a room of one's own. Having someone to take care of your kids so you can drag a pen across the page is a room of one's own.

A zulo is the antithesis of a room of one's own. A zulo is a park bench. It's a borrowed computer. It's a bathroom and a rooftop. A zulo is where the dispossessed write. Those who work four shifts. Those who don't have anyone to rock their kid to sleep so they can drag a pencil across the page. A zulo is a sewer, a border.

Ziga didn't know that I wanted to be a writer, of course, or that I write. But she saw a rage in my eyes, that rage shared by those who live in the sewers. The Chicana feminist Chela Sandoval calls this mutual recognition among marginalized creatures the methodology of the oppressed; Audre Lorde, deep looking. It is the capacity to recognize the mark of marginalization and the mark of resistance in others. So, she knew I was living in a zulo and that I was going to emerge from it.

And I do know what I want. I want to be a writer. But not just any kind of writer. I don't want to be a writer who contemplates catastrophes from a café in a leafy neighborhood with postcard-worthy streets, untouched by the horror because she merely observes it in the pages of the police blotter. I don't want to be a writer who goes abroad to specialize in creative writing and whose novels have perfect structures. I don't want to be a writer praised by critics because she whitens marginalized characters. I don't want to write about whores who are avid readers or about drug addicts who get high at ayahuasca ceremonies.

FEMINISM WITHOUT A ROOM OF ONE'S OWN 59

I don't think it's wrong to specialize in creative writing or to write in a studio in an upper-middle-class neighborhood. There are thousands of paths, but that one isn't mine. Mine is at the edge of the abyss. I'm at home in a zulo. I emerged from a zulo, and my political commitment is to write from and for the place where I come to a boil.

My mom was raised in a community of three thousand souls in the mountains of Jalisco. The streets were unpaved and the houses had tiled roofs in that town where women grew fond of the pigs to be slaughtered for the May festivities and raised them like children, y que se chingue el guateque. Where everyone knew everyone and everyone knew what everyone was up to and gossiped about everyone else with the same intensity as they supported each other when times were tough. The barrio was the closest thing my mother ever found to her community, so I grew up in the barrio. I grew up between dirty walls and danzantes and murals of the Virgin of Guadalupe on every corner. Experiencing violence and inequality and marginalization firsthand left its mark. As Canserbero says, el barrio no pasó en vano.

My old lady firmly believed that you could climb the social hierarchy chingándole machín. Work your way up. Get paid. Work your way up. Get paid. Get paid. And one sign of our family working its way up was enrolling me in a Catholic school, which was a status symbol at the time. Since I am what's known in race studies as "white-passing"—which only means not being a racialized person, that is, Indigenous or Black or Asian—my mother thought that my social life at school was already half settled. But she was wrong. My zip code was enough for me to be on the receiving end of all sorts of classist discrimination. I wasn't the kind of girl whose hair got pulled by boys to get her attention, they never hid under the stairs to catch a glimpse of my panties, and they never tried to lift up my skirt. I didn't experience violence involving sexist discrimination or misogyny in my early childhood. I was the girl they called ratchet, naca trash, corriente, what's she doing in our school if she's so poor. My initial otherness was not being a woman, it was being naca.

At a young age—there are even feminist theorists who argue that it begins when the doctor utters the phrase *it's a girl*—women (from a certain context) are indoctrinated into a series of inflexible stereotypes and expectations about how to be a little woman. Recent books like *Brave, Not Perfect* and *Rage Becomes Her* address the issue of how the "feminine" socialization that tells us to be demuremodestperfectclean sweet princesses affects our psychosocial development. And how women who don't fit into the mold of the sweet princess are pathologized and labeled bossyirritabletyrannical and evil. This debate isn't new to feminism. In *The Second Sex*, Simone de Beauvoir extensively analyzed the differences between the way female children and male children are raised, as well as how this affects the development of an individual's personality, their way of being in the world, and the way the world treats them. Although these analyses emerged from white feminism and speak to the experiences of white, white-passing, or whitened women/girls, they do define the socialization of many women. I wouldn't call it feminine socialization, though, but white/whitened feminine socialization.

I never identified with hegemonic femininity: I liked riding my bicycle and taking toads home and playing fighting games at the arcade. And I hated long hair, ribbons, dresses, patent leather shoes. Not to mention bathing. But this wasn't something I could say to the other girls in my class because to fit in a little, I'd have to pretend I liked playing with Barbies: once again, white/whitened femininity isn't just sexist, but involves

FEMINISM WITHOUT A ROOM OF ONE'S OWN   61

questions of race and class. It's not enough to be a sweet princess, you have to be a sweet princess with the manners of a colonial aristocrat. Although I never identified with the colonial model of the aristocrat's daughter, I was socialized in white/whitened femininity and my first years at school were marked by my silence in the face of my classmates' hurtful words. I swallowed my rage and cried when I got home. I suffered in silence. I felt so ashamed that I couldn't even tell anyone people called me poor and naca. I knew there was nothing wrong with being naca and impoverished, but it hurt me that they used it as an insult.

MY LUCK CHANGED when I drank an entire bottle of bathroom air freshener in a tantrum because my dad didn't let me adopt a stray cat. He took me to the barrio pharmacy, a tiny drugstore that made ends meet by offering doctor's appointments for twenty pesos and selling prescription medicine to the neighborhood cholos. There I met Ivone, the doctor's stepdaughter. We immediately clicked. She also did all kinds of radical things to get what she wanted, like drinking bleach. She loved playing kick the can and Tazos, and she would skim two pesos from the tortilla money for arcade games. She invited me over for a sleepover one weekend and that sleepover marked the start of long seasons in which I lived at her house and only went home for short visits, leaving as soon as I arrived.

Ivone lived on the outskirts of town. Her neighbors were drug users, sex workers, teenagers in trouble with the law, and a Rarámuri family. There were two rooms in her home: one with the stove, the fridge, and a little table; the other with two beds, a cot, and a couch. There were bedbugs. Lots of bedbugs. Ivone was one of the rich kids in the vecindad because they had their own bathroom, while almost everyone else had to share. She introduced me to her friends, who became my friends. They were the daughters of construction workers and sex workers and domestic workers and used clothing vendors at the tianguis. They were all incredibly fun and empathetic and supportive; I loved that I could relax around them. I didn't have to pretend to be someone I wasn't with them or live up to inflexible gender models. I could be dirty and rude and grumpy, and nobody would judge me for it.

During my childhood and adolescence, I spent my mornings with upper- or upper-middle-class girls who were white or undergoing the process of being whitened and who ate with refined manners and never used any words worse than tonta. Girls who never shouted, who held it all in. Who became passive-aggressive from holding so much in. Who may have been truly hateful, classist princesses, but who were princesses nonetheless. And I spent my afternoons with brown morras who danced cumbia and sat to watch danzantes rehearse while they sloppily devoured duros preparados. Morras in dirty clothes because they had been working at the tianguis or washing three loads of laundry.

Here I make the distinction between girls and morras not only to mark a race and class divide, but also as the seed of some theoretical contributions I will share later on, taken from the work of the feminist María Lugones. She argues that "woman" is white: that those who are Black and of color are always considered to be others, like beasts. But I make this distinction from a place of belonging and vindication. I'm a morra, and later I'll become a doña. Being a señora is such a drag.

This may seem anecdotal, but it's not. It's political. Because what you experience in your childhood and adolescence shapes your character and because each time someone asks me why I see things that other feminists don't, how I manage to reach

FEMINISM WITHOUT A ROOM OF ONE'S OWN 63

certain conclusions or have a certain mental clarity or philosophical pulchritude, I reply: *porque me sobra barrio*. It's true. Those of us who emerge from our zulos, those who know that inequality can be explained by noodle soup, have a mental clarity that doesn't come from books. We have the mental clarity that comes from rifártela en la vida loca. It'll never be the same to learn about social inequality from reading Marx while eating three meals a day as from working twelve hours to eat two. Lived experience is lived experience. It's not anecdotal, it's political, because we've swallowed the tale of whiteness and bourgeois aspirationalism so fully that the spaces we vindicate always have to do with what grants us prestige. That's why we brag about reading Cortázar but not *El libro vaquero*. That's why we brag about eating a designer ramen on social media, but not a bolillo con crema. We brag about our luxuries and triumphs, but not our defeats and dark places. We brag about everything that grants us whiteness because, of course, whiteness has its benefits under a racist system.

I'm interested in vindicating myself through otherness. Through a writing ritual that doesn't involve whisky but gorditas de chicharrón verde and Coca-Cola in a glass bottle, through debt that never seems to get any smaller, not even working four shifts a day. I'm interested in vindicating the lessons I learned working at the tianguis, the factory, and the call center. Having to borrow money to buy kibble for my little beasts, watching horrors unfold while sitting on a bench in a barrio bravo instead of reading about them in the newspaper at a fashionable café. Taking three months to finish this essay because I had to pawn my laptop. It's important to me that you know I lived in the barrio and that I came to understand that the world is muy hijo de perro for women, especially for those from zulos, as I sat under a mural of the Virgin of Guadalupe and listened to my friend tell me about how her uncle abused her, Los Temerarios playing in the background. I'm interested in vindicating the fact that my husband and his family, which is now my family, lived in a cinderblock house forever under construction and it was in this family living on the margins that I found a refuge from the world's cruelty. I didn't learn the multifarious nature of oppression and the many faces of violence from books but from the barrio and that's why I'm interested in positioning this knowledge beyond academic exoticism. I speak from this place in honor of my childhood, my friends, my family, and in protest against those who criminalize, bestialize, and mock these corners of the world through their classism, but also as part of my commitment to betraying my own whiteness and bourgeois aspirationalism.

In the barrio, I learned that inequality can be explained by noodle soup. Marxists and others on the left argue that there are only two social classes: those above and those below, and that the bourgeoisie are "those who control the means of production." I call this bourgeois fragility, the inability of the privileged social classes to acknowledge their class privilege under a theoretical argument. I endorse the concept that the bourgeoisie are the middle class and above; when I say "bourgeoisie," I'm not only referring to those who control the means of production, but also those who are comfortably middle class and upper middle class.

But let's get back to the idea of the soup. Allow me to explain: Ivone's mom worked outside the city on the weekends and would leave us twenty pesos for food, which Ivone used to buy tomato bouillon cubes and pasta to make noodle soup. Other friends from the barrio made it with tomatoes and onions and pasta. And the nanny of the only girl I befriended at school—because who cooks in a home is also political—made it with chicken stock and tomatoes and onions and tomato bouillon and vegetables. Inequality is multifarious because so are oppressions and the place you occupy in the economic model and how and what and who is cooking a noodle soup can tell us a lot about the place you occupy in the matrix of oppressions. This may seem obvious, especially if you've experienced precarity, but there are some who don't understand. Like those who earn more than ten thousand pesos a month and say they're impoverished because people can only be either rich or poor. And who are surprised when you explain it to them with noodle soup but then continue denying their privilege. Food is a right, and rights aren't privileges, they'll tell you. Rights are rights, no argument there, but you need economic and racial privilege to access them. The first problem we have in accepting our privilege is that we think the problem lies in how we exercise it to benefit from it, but we rarely reflect on how it de facto benefits us. The second problem is that whenever someone points out that we have privilege—for example, class privilege—instead of accepting that we have a privileged salary, we throw ourselves on the ground and cry and shout, "But I'm not Carlos Slim." No. It doesn't work like that; your degree of privilege is analyzed based on who you are and who is at a comparative disadvantage to you, while your drama has to do with who has more than you. No, Anasofi, you aren't Carlos Slim, but you earn triple what 80 percent of Mexicans earn and your life experiences, purchasing power, and class socialization are closer to Carlos Slim than the woman selling seeds outside the metro station. Let's abort white fragility, but also class fragility.

It's not about asking for forgiveness for being white or for earning fifteen thousand pesos a month, but we also shouldn't banalize the discussion with a strawman that mocks those who point out our privilege. Nor is it about depoliticizing analyses of the matrix of oppressions by turning them into an Oppression Olympics. It's about acknowledging our privilege, accepting it, understanding how we benefit from it and how the system benefits us, so that we can manage that privilege in the most ethical way possible—we can't ethically manage something we don't even acknowledge exists.

My friendship with Ivone se fue a la verga because she got married at thirteen. Yes, thirteen. In zulos, morras see hooking up with their jaino as a method of emancipation. At home, they do the laundry for their entire family. They cook for their entire family. They raise their siblings and nephews, and it makes sense for them to start their own family and only take care of their viejo. So I was left alone with Leticia. Leticia was my friend for two more years and got married at fifteen. Today she's a happy housewife, and I'm happy that she's happy.

If I learned that inequality is a noodle soup from Ivone, from Leticia I learned that "feminine socialization" is a matter for girls, not morras. Leticia gave me my first lesson in feminine socialization outside the canons of whiteness: *don't swallow your rage.* One day, I told her that I went the long way home from school because there was a morra from the vecindad on the avenue who talked shit whenever I walked by and it scared me and I didn't know how to react. *¡Eres bien culo, güera!* she said. *If you don't throw down, she'll fuck with you forever. The next time you go that way, you drop your bag, tie your hair back, and say: ¡Véngase, perra! And you beat the shit out of her.* I was astonished. Nothing about peace and love. Nothing about how I'm fantastic and how I should just ignore her. She not only had the audacity to tell me to violently express my rage, but she even threatened me: *If I hear you took the long way home or she said something to you and you didn't fight back, then I'll* *kick the shit out of you for being such a pussy!* I later realized that this was a form of socialization. Her mom told me the same thing: *I'll kick your ass if you let them walk all over you.* Her aunts affectionately called each other bitches. The girls from my school called me baby; Lety called me a cunt. The girls from my school covered their mouths when they burped; Lety and Laura and Lupita and I competed to see who could burp the loudest. The mothers of the girls from my school were tired of their husbands and of being housewives and the doñas raised in the barrio were working at the tianguis and on the corner and in the factories and washing the clothes of the exasperated mothers of the girls from school. Do you still doubt that the femininity of the polite daughter of the colony is the product of whiteness and the coloniality of being? Take a look at the stereotype of the angry Black woman.

This was the context of my childhood and adolescence, one of working-class women who are always in public spaces. Women who theorize as they dig through the latest heaps of used clothes at the pacas. Free women who go swimming in bra and panties. Women who'll break your face if you're passive-aggressive to them. Women who'll tell you straight out *¡Chingas a tu puta madre y vete a la verga!* if you upset them. And call you *pinche perra*, affectionately. I didn't understand what feminism was all about. I didn't understand the feminism of women with a room of their own because I emerged from a zulo.

THE GENEALOGY OF RAGE

I intend to make a series of specific critiques of feminism with a room of one's own or white feminism or hegemonic or radical feminism, but before I do, I'd like to briefly review Feminism™ so that we'll be working from the same conceptual framework and basic theoretical foundation. Let's start with definitions. What is feminism? Feminism is "the radical notion that women are people." Feminism is a set of theories, agendas, vindications, and praxes for the liberation/empowerment/emancipation of women.

Many men (and women), feeling quite intellectual, ask: *If feminism seeks equity, why is it called feminism and not egalitarianism? If you want equity, why not call it humanism?* The answer may seem obvious, but for many people it isn't because the emancipation of women has not yet been consummated. Because there is NO context in which being a woman does not mean being subjected to sexist violence, machismo, discrimination, and oppressions when the sex/gender system intersects with class and racialization. Because in Mexico nine women are murdered each day, many of them under the age of nine. Femicide victims are raped and degraded in a thousand and one ways before being killed. A rape occurs every five seconds. Sexual harassment begins, on average, at the age of seven. Abortion is punished with prison time. In some countries, morras who are menstruating are sent to special huts and many die from snakebites. From clitorectomies. From selective abortions when the fetus is female. Forced marriages under the age of twelve. Having to carry pregnancies to term that were the product of rape at the age of ten. Transfemicides. The expulsion of Indigenous nations from their territories. Forced sterilizations of racialized and impoverished women. Feminism is called feminism because it seeks to adjust the balance in favor of women, a balance that has historically been tilted against us, and still is. Besides—equal? To whom? There's not even equality among men.

One of the other objections to feminism is the idea that feminism was perrón back in the day, when feminists fought

FEMINISM WITHOUT A ROOM OF ONE'S OWN   69

for the right to vote and the right to an education, whereas feminists today fight to grow out their armpit hair and upload photos of their bloody menstrual cups. Allow me to explain it with apples and oranges: Feminism involves theory, agenda, praxis, and vindication. Fighting to secure access to legal abortion forms part of an agenda and raising awareness that menstrual blood is neither impure nor dirty nor stinky is a vindication. Surprise! They're not mutually exclusive. To explain the differences between theory, agenda, praxis, and vindication, I'll use the waves of feminism as an example. I don't agree with the organization of feminist genealogy into waves because it erases the contributions of Black women and women of color, but it seems to be a useful systematization for explaining these concepts.

What is a feminist agenda? The feminist agenda answers *what* questions, and to explain it, I'll use the example of the first wave. The feminists of the first wave focused on the idea that women are also citizens and, therefore, had legal rights. Alongside these statements comes an agenda. Once it was shown that women are citizens—ergo they should have the same rights as men—they specified what they wanted, what they demanded, what we needed in order to emancipate ourselves. The agenda of the first wave can practically be reduced to women's suffrage.

The first wave is the one that's most commonly cited by the detractors of feminism to argue that *those* were the ones who were chingonas y rifadas. The ones who were asking for equal rights. Their demands were what we call an agenda: being able to vote, get divorced, have legal protections within marriage, the right to own and inherit property, reproductive justice, respect for one's gender identity, civil marriage between lesbians, spaces free from sexual harassment, and the abolition of slavery, among other elemental liberties—this is the feminist agenda. And for each victory in the struggle, for each point we can cross off the agenda, there are ten that have yet to be accomplished. The feminist agenda is still focused on basic human rights and freedoms.

To respond to those who say that feminists back in the day were chidas and feminists today are nothing but a bunch of loud hysterics who march naked: In Mexico, countless women se la rifan to secure specific changes in urgent situations. GIRE, a feminist human rights organization that seeks to guarantee sexual and reproductive rights through the legal system. Sabuesos Guerreras, an NGO dedicated to searching for the mortal remains of the disappeared by excavating mass graves with expert training. Nuestras Hijas de Regreso a Casa, which fights against femicide and accompanies families who are looking for their daughters. Equis: Justicia Para Las Mujeres, which works to improve the legal system and does advocacy work in prisons. There are women fighting against forced sterilization in Chiapas right now. Against the theft of sacred lands. Against police violence in the barrio. There are morras helping others abort outside the law. There are morras fighting custody battles and demanding child support payments. Giving self-defense classes in middle schools on the urban periphery. The feminists of our day aren't so different from the ones in days past; the difference is that, as we fight in highly concrete ways for women's liberation, we also take photos of our hairy armpits as part of a vindication.

The traditional (hegemonic) genealogy of the theorization of sexual difference and the problematization of the inequalities between men and women we know as feminism were inaugurated by the publication of *Declaration of the Rights of Woman and of the Female Citizen* by Olympe de Gouges and

A Vindication of the Rights of Woman by Mary Wollstonecraft. The publication of these two texts, along with the suffragette movement, is known as the first wave. If we speak of feminism as a political position, we then have to say that it began with the Enlightenment. Nevertheless, the struggle for the emancipation of women didn't begin with white and European women and there were already many examples of insurgency, rebellion, and praxis that problematized the oppression of women, fought to emancipate them, and allowed them to escape from traditional roles. Before all rebellion and emancipation and search for liberation was called feminism, there were rebel women fighting against all forms of oppression. There were witches, shamans, and Black women founding quilombos. The struggle against social hierarchy precedes feminism.

During the first wave, differences began to appear between middle- and upper-class women, working-class women, and racialized women. The first wanted the right to vote, the second wanted labor rights and wage equality, and the third wanted the abolition of slavery. Sojourner Truth, a Black feminist rarely mentioned in the traditional genealogies of feminism, delivered a speech titled "Ain't I a Woman?" that made clear the differences between white women and others. Over the course of this text, I will refer to these differences as being between the feminists with a room of their own and zulo feminists.

> Agenda = What rights, freedoms, abolitions,
> or emancipations do we still need to secure?
> The agenda responds to the *what* question.

The second wave of feminism began in the seventies and represented a boom in feminist theory; it was in this era that the "great classics of feminism" were written. Theory is that which, through intellectual exercises, research, observation, and reflection, allows us to problematize, question, and seek explanations for and consequences of hierarchized and differentiated treatment and the differences between women in all their varied contexts, life experiences, and intersections of class and race. The first wave focused on legal inequalities and the second wave on structural inequalities and the search for *whys*. Marriage was problematized as an instrument of oppression. The family as an instrument of slavery. Maternity as a cultural construct. The right to abortion was discussed for the first time. Family planning. Women as objects of consumption. The porn industry as hate speech against women. *The Second Sex. Our Blood. The Feminine Mystique. The Dialectic of Sex. Sexual Politics.* The theoretical contributions were many: Andrea Dworkin asking for twenty-four hours without a rape. Analyses of how, throughout history, women's work has gone unremunerated in the name of love. Love as the opiate of women. Historical materialism and the Marxist dialectic were translated into feminist terms: for there to be an oppressed class, you need an oppressor. Women as a sex class oppressed by an oppressor class: men. The origins of the patriarchy were analyzed. It was said that it arose when the plow replaced the hoe. No, that it was when men discovered the male role in procreation. No, it was when the alphabet replaced the goddess because activities associated with the left hemisphere of the brain began to be valued more highly. No, it was when Prometheus brought fire to men.

In the second wave, two great branches of feminism emerged: equality feminism and difference feminism. Equality feminism argues that women and men are essentially the same and that the only thing that makes us "different" is a differentiated upbringing. It also argues that women are capable of doing anything that men do and that the goal should be for girls

FEMINISM WITHOUT A ROOM OF ONE'S OWN   73

and boys to be raised with the same permissions and the same
limitations. Difference feminism, in turn, argues that human
females and human males are clearly not the same and that the
problem lies not in difference itself, but in the reading given to
that difference; the solution would then not be to imitate men,
but to vindicate the feminine and stop using sexual difference
as an excuse for hierarchization. The second wave establishes
feminist theory.

> Theory: To problematize, discover the how,
> when, why, and what.
> Agenda: To identify a problem and
> propose a solution.

While first wave feminism exemplified the foundations of
a feminist agenda (in a biased fashion, to be sure) and the
second wave did so for theory, then the third is the wave of
vindications. Although there have been major theoretical
contributions—such as queer theory and its extraordinary
exponents like Butler and Preciado, Diana "Pornoterrorista"
Torres, Despentes, and Itziar Ziga—they all reach the conclusion that it's important to vindicate that which is considered
abject. There is a powerful reappropriation of slurs. It's important to discuss sexual orientation as an identity because puto is
the last word dozens of maricones hear before being murdered.
It's important to draw vulvas everywhere because the vulva
has been the invisible sex for centuries. We have to discuss
menstruation because there are young people who are excluded
from their communities when they're bleeding. We need to
discuss body diversity because, for years, we have only ever
seen hegemonic models of beauty that ravaged our self-esteem.
We need to talk about how fat women are beautiful because
thousands of women die from eating disorders each year.

Naturally, these identitarian movements must seem stupid if you're a handsome white middle- or upper-class heterosexual man and you don't have a functional diversity because you're hegemonic and the norm and standard. This also applies to women. Especially conventionally beautiful, white, middle-class feminists who say there is one sole feminism, rather than many: the feminism that fights oppression. Singular, as if there were only one oppression. These feminists with a room of their own argue that Black feminism isn't necessary because dividing women into Black and white only separates us. Yes, the people who say that identitarian movements aren't important are the same ones who say *I don't see Black or white or jotos or lesbians or men or women: I just see people.* I'd like to tell them *fuck off, fatherfucker,* but it's better to cite Michelle Haimoff: "Black women wake up in the morning, look in the mirror, and see Black women. White women wake up in the morning, look in the mirror, and see women. White men wake up in the morning, look in the mirror, and see human beings."

In the third wave, movements arose to defend diverse bodies and LGBTTTQI+ identities. After all, being a lesbian isn't just a sexual orientation, it's a site of resistance and a political position. These movements show the importance of naming oneself through otherness—through the powerful reappropriation of slurs. It's the struggle of faggots and trannies and dykes and whores and freaks and coloreds and fatties to exist through difference, without this difference being translated into discrimination. In the third wave, we talk about orgasms because only one in every ten heterosexual women has a satisfying sex life. We talk about armpit hair because hairy men have spent centuries making us feel dirty for being human beings who have body hair and stretch marks and cellulite. But it turns out that what can be vindicated for some can't be vindicated for others. For

FEMINISM WITHOUT A ROOM OF ONE'S OWN   75

many white feminists, marching naked is a powerful rebellion against the prudishness in which they were raised, yet nudity is not necessarily a vindication or an act of rebellion for Black feminists. As the Black theorist Yuderkys Espinosa has argued, Black women have always been naked, whether as objects of study in museums and human zoos or in the racist/misogynist imaginary that exoticizes them. For Black women, afros and headwraps and braids and the color of their skin and their big and powerful bodies are to be vindicated. Everything associated with their race and all the reasons for which they have been bestialized and marginalized and abused. Muslim women, especially those living in the West, vindicate the use of the burqa and the hijab. For them, it's not just about religion, but culture and identity and resistance because they are harassed and abused in terrible ways for wearing them. Other women vindicate their monolid eyes. Others, their stretch marks or the nudity of their imperfect bodies. What you vindicate is where you were hurt, where you were insulted. Whatever is used to call you dirty and evil and crazy and slutty and dark and butch and queer and undeserving of rights. That site of abjection is your site of vindication. Drawing vulvas and uploading photos of menstrual blood and stretch marks and body hair have the goal of raising awareness and normalizing and destigmatizing.

The feminists with a room of their own always want to go one step further in their critiques on the belief that they're getting down to the root of things. So they criticize those *poor creatures* for defending the hijab, because how can you defend a symbol of oppression? They criticize Black women for *moving their ass in such a filthy way. How dare they dance reggaeton like that! Why do they hypersexualize themselves so?* It's very curious to me that, whenever other feminists have asked me what I think about women who hypersexualize themselves, their examples are always Black women. Women who are scorned for expressing a sexuality other than that of a conservative white woman. Black women and women of color know themselves to be sexually powerful and have used dance since ancestral times to connect with the energy of their forebears and find the power and resistance that dwells therein. They're not dancing dirty; you're just judging them through your moral standards.

Those feminists who get down to the root also criticize fat women for uploading nudes because *how can they upload photos of their fat asses, what's gotten into them, that's not feminism*. Nothing that gets a man hard is feminism, they say. They argue that body diversity movements fall into the capitalist trap of turning bodies into objects to be consumed, that we should abolish the mandate to be beautiful rather than expanding the concept of the beautiful. Oh? And how do we abolish the beauty mandate? Because, to me, as long as there are women who look in the mirror and want to smash it because they feel ugly, the solution isn't to tell them that beauty doesn't exist, but rather that there are many ways of being beautiful. It's more practical. That's why representation is important. Little girls receive a message of power when they read magazines and watch TV shows where they see fat and Black and "ugly" women and women who don't fit into beauty standards and who triumph and are powerful and do great things. Saying that we must abolish the beauty mandate is nothing more than rhetoric. The racist and classist critiques of the vindications of others are known as purplewashing. Purplewashing is when feminism is used as an excuse to reproduce other systems of oppression. Purplewashing is saying, *Silly Black woman, stop dancing like that, you're hurting the rest of us.* You can go ahead and keep doing it. But don't say you're being critical or feminist, you're just being basic, racist, and classist.

> Vindication = to remove the stigma from that
> which is othered or considered abject.

Finally, we get to praxis. Feminist praxis is action. Praxis is easily confused with friendship, but embracing your girlfriends isn't feminist praxis, it's simply an expression of affection. Praxis is accompanying abortions, covering the city with posters of disappeared women, denouncing racism, and making your space an antiracist one. Praxis is organizing workshops with women in contact with the prison system, giving legal advice to women suffering violence or undergoing a divorce, opening a community kitchen for the LGBTTTQI+ community; praxis is donating condoms and lube to organized sex workers, praxis is respecting the pronouns of trans and nonbinary people. Praxis is putting your body on the line. Marches aren't praxis, they're a strategy.

IN THIS BRIEF history we notice that, in the genealogy divided into waves, only the feminism with a room of one's own is visible. These divisions overlook Black women and women of color. They were always present. During the second wave, great works by Angela Davis and bell hooks and Audre Lorde were published, along with anthologies of Black and Chicana and Third World feminism, but they don't appear in the chronologies because the narrative is dominated by feminism with a room of one's own and erases those who emerge from zulos. This, too, is racism.

Through my epistemological approach, feminism is divided into two major groups: the feminism that calls us all to unite around the oppression of having a vulva, which I call white feminism or feminism with a room of one's own, and the feminism that theorizes and generates agendas and alliances through the concept of the matrix of oppressions, zulo feminism.

RADICAL FEMINISM:
THE MAYONNAISE OF FEMINISM

The first time I saw the word *feminism* used to refer to a movement that sought the emancipation of women was when I googled the word *abortion*. I had an unwanted pregnancy and wanted to know what my options were. I found those options in feminism, along with information and accompaniment. So I wanted to know who these women were who told me *everything's going to be fine* from across the ocean while I aborted outside the laws of god and man. I looked up a basic reading list on the internet and at the library. I read *The Second Sex*, and it struck me as an extraordinary analysis. The trouble came with *The Feminine Mystique, The Dialectic of Sex*, and *Sexual Politics*. I understood their analysis on the origins of women's oppression, and I understood the issues they raised, but I couldn't empathize with those issues because I came from another context: a zulo.

In my context, the dichotomy between the public and the private didn't exist; the women around me had always been working on the street and in the fields and in the houses of other women. I didn't understand the authors' exasperation with their husbands, either, because very few women I knew were married, and the ones who were faced a problem much more serious than tedium: femicidal violence. I didn't understand why they were asking to go back to work when all the

FEMINISM WITHOUT A ROOM OF ONE'S OWN

women who came before me, even prior to the sixties, had worked in both private space—the family—as well as in public space—the fields. I read about a femininity built on fragility and sexual modesty and remembered Lety's aunts going swimming in their underwear, not caring that everyone could see their nipples and pubic hair once they got wet. Fragility and weakness? But my mom carried up to twenty liters of water on her head from the river to our house and my girlfriends assembled their heavy tianguis stalls by themselves. I felt how people from the Global South feel whenever they read about the problems of white upper-class Europeans. I didn't understand feminism. Not then. That feminism didn't reflect either the femininity or the needs of women like my sisters and friends, not to mention my own needs. Feminism with a room of one's own wasn't revealing any truths about life to me and it wasn't solving my problems.

This is not a coincidence. The vast majority of theoreticians who are legitimized by academia or who are promoted as having laid the basis for feminist theory are white (or white-passing or mestiza or whitened) and middle- or upper-class feminists with a room of their own who have enough time and money and other women working for them to be able to accumulate cultural capital and epistemic privileges and theorize from there. Theorizing from a place of privilege can generate interesting contributions, especially if it involves a project of liberation, but it runs the risk of generating analyses through privilege because we see everything through our privilege and context. If your context is being a white upper-class woman with a university education who has never experienced racism and never hustled to put food on the table, it's natural that your concerns will be ennui and access to high-ranking positions and the right to vote and the number of women who are published each year. But there are women in zulos whose vital necessities are a plate of food and better wages and finding time to raise their children and protecting them from police violence.

So we can say that white feminism is theoretically important, but that it lacks many perspectives and formulates agendas that only benefit those women who have the most and not those who have the least. Who cleans up the shards of the glass ceilings broken by white women?

I may be full of social resentment, but I don't hate the contributions of white feminism or feminism with a room of one's own or radical feminism, although I do consider many of the feminists that gave them form to be my antithesis. I appreciate their contributions because many of them laid the basis for theories that were vital to internal debates in the struggle for our rights, above all the powerful thesis that the personal is political. But it's important to make it clear that the concepts we have unquestioningly inherited, such as "patriarchy," or the slogans we repeat, such as "unite around a shared oppression," or the books we consider to be essential, such as *The Female Eunuch*, have achieved this status because of the de facto visibility of the women who wrote them, a visibility associated with being at the top of social hierarchies. And, of course, the fact that we don't know concepts like "the matrix of oppressions" or "the sex/gender system" or books like *This Bridge Called My Back* has to do with what is known in decolonial studies as the coloniality of knowledge, which is nothing other than the fact that knowledge that is generated by white people who inhabit the First World is knowledge that becomes epistemologically hegemonic, while the knowledge that arises in the Global South or from people of color is not taken seriously. White women with a room of their own write theories that are international while Black women write to divide the movement, they say.

When I studied philosophy, the fathers of epistemologies and hermeneutics and ontologies and critical apparatuses told me *think, therefore you are*. But then I found my gurus of color and they told me *feel and you'll be free*.

IN THE SECOND wave, the most "critical" current of feminism was born: radical feminism. Many people understand radical feminism to mean those feminists who spray paint the walls and protest naked over hate crimes against women. The radicals are the feminists who openly say that they *do* hate men and quote Valerie Solanas. But that isn't radical feminism, that's a praxis and a series of individual positions. Radical feminism is a theoretical current that affirms that there are two classes, the oppressed and the oppressor, and that gender is the tool of oppression. Radical feminism is heir to Marxism and dialectics and historical materialism, so it argues that women are an oppressed sex class. What makes us a "class" is that we share what Karina Vergara Sánchez calls "assumed reproductive capacity" and specific sexual characteristics—that is, a materiality. Radical feminism claims that the basis of oppression is sex. And that the tool of oppression is gender. And it concludes that we must abolish gender in order to secure women's liberation.

I studied philosophy, so the structure of an argument is very important to me. Ever since I heard the phrase "sex is the material basis of oppression," the premise seemed problematic. This formulation argues—unintentionally—that oppression does have a justification, and that justification is sexual difference. It's a poorly formulated premise: when we reason poorly, we conceptualize poorly and, as Celia Amorós says, when we conceptualize poorly, we do politics poorly. The problem doesn't lie in our genitals or in our assumed reproductive capacity or in the vulva. The problem lies in attributing our otherness to biological difference. The oppression of women has no basis or justification; what it has is a structure: hierarchization. The problem is hierarchization, not the biological fact. It's not the materiality, it's the interpretation of that materiality. Oppression has no material basis; it has an ideological structure. And there isn't one single hierarchization, there are several and they all intertwine.

When I argue it's a fallacy (or several) to say that sex is the basis of oppression, I'm always bombarded with questions: *How do they decide whose clitoris to mutilate? How do they decide who to kill in sex-selective abortions?* Naturally, when deciding who to rape, rapists select their victim through the immediateness of sex (or an immediate sexualized reading). But it's not sex itself that kills or justifies killing, it's the interpretation given to this biological fact, it's hierarchization and devaluation. There's an enormous semantic and symbolic difference between saying "sex is the basis of oppression" and saying "oppression has no basis or justification." Oppression is articulated in the hierarchization that occurs through sexist/racist/classist interpretations of biological facts. Once again, when we reason poorly, we do politics poorly. How can we accept the plausibility of a theoretical project that's based on a false premise, or that's "poorly formulated" at best? Why do we unthinkingly adopt these theoretical contributions if they're highly problematic, down to their very syntax? Because they were developed by feminists with a room of their own who are legitimized per se by the coloniality of knowledge, even if what they say is bullshit.

IN THEORY, radical feminists seek to abolish everything that implies the exploitation of women: marriage and pornography

FEMINISM WITHOUT A ROOM OF ONE'S OWN   83

and prostitution and maternity. Yet they have strong cognitive and theoretical and ethical biases and they specifically focus on those topics that make them uncomfortable, like sex work. There is a certain degree of injustice, inequity, or exploitation in all relationships that imply the exchange of labor for money or cultural or political capital, but if you see exploitation in sex work and not in cleaning bathrooms full of shit and menstrual blood, and you want to abolish the first but don't really care about the second, then you not only have to revise your ethical values but also your debate skills, because you have to be very intellectually and ethically clumsy to think that one is patriarchal exploitation and the other is full of poetry. It may seem harmless or even ethically correct to seek the abolition of prostitution, but what you decide to put your energy into, what you denounce, what you want to abolish, what you demand, and what you define as your agenda all speak to whether you're a feminist with a room of your own or a feminist from a zulo.

Radical feminism aims to abolish everything that implies exploitation but sees gender as the primordial violence. It understands gender as the set of roles and characteristics and qualities and impositions and limitations violently imposed on the sex class of women. It believes that femininity is a tool that men have used to domesticate us. Femininity is a male fetish and fantasy imposed on women, it argues, so we have to tear down femininity and gender. It takes the abolition of gender to mean that there will no longer be things for men and things for women, just whatever your ass feels like. Men can put on makeup and women can shave their heads. Women can be mathematicians and men can be cooks. These contributions are important because they represented the first definitions of the patriarchy and gender and women as a sex class. But they shouldn't go unquestioned, they don't represent stone tablets of women's liberation, much less dogmas, because they're actually fairly myopic and problematic. For example, they define the patriarchy as a megastructure of cultural and symbolic and economic and political systems that favor men at the expense of women. "Women as a class" argues that women are a sex class that is oppressed for their sex and that men are the oppressor class and that gender is the mechanism of oppression. Meanwhile, Black feminists and feminists of color have been critiquing the concepts of patriarchy and gender, and even oppression, since the seventies. They've spoken up in texts like *White Woman Listen!* but it seems we haven't been, because we keep repeating nonsense about how all women are oppressed.

Because feminists with a room of their own see sexual hierarchization as the greatest oppression, they spend all their time trying to eliminate everything they see as being implicated in that oppression and that is why they solely focus on topics that have to do with vulvas. Radical theory taught them that the dialectic of oppression is primordially sexual. Women who emerge from their zulos, on the other hand, also fight against racism and classism because their lived experience has taught them that sexual hierarchies are connected to racial and social hierarchies.

> When we theorize poorly, we propose myopic agendas
> that don't represent the needs of all women.

Zulo feminists have problematized all the theories of radical feminism. For example, they have criticized how white feminism has turned the concept of the patriarchy into THE macrostructure. The problem with the term "patriarchy" is that it's limited in denouncing the structural violence experienced by women because there isn't only one form of sex/gender

FEMINISM WITHOUT A ROOM OF ONE'S OWN   85

oppression, but many. It's not solely constructed through sexual hierarchization and it's not true that all women are oppressed. The concept of the patriarchy leaves out oppressions due to class and race, which are connected to oppressions due to sex/gender. Patriarchy is an inexact concept because, if we're being strict, an oppression exclusively due to sex/gender does not exist outside its interactions with hierarchies of class and race, because many freedoms that are restricted for women can be bought. Which ones? Abortion, for example. No, the patriarchy is not an enormous monster sitting at a wooden table, raising his glass: *Here's to oppressing women.* Nor is it a kraken, with class and race and sexual orientation as its tentacles. These analogies used by radical feminists make it clear that they do see a hierarchy of oppressions and that, for them, the primary oppression or monster is the dichotomous relationship between the sexes, while those articulated through class and race are incidental.

To fix the theoretical myopy of the term "patriarchy," racialized feminists have put forward concepts such as the matrix of oppressions and patriarchal relationships. The term "patriarchal relationships" is more exact because it situates the hierarchization between the sexes as one of several systems of oppression, but not the only one or the most important. Patriarchal relationships are connected with other social hierarchizations because class and race and sexual orientation and gender identity and functional diversity are not mere variables or complements, but violent hierarchizations in themselves. And though there's no such thing as an Oppression Olympics, because they all intertwine in what's known as the intersection of oppressions, it's definitely not the same to be an upper-class white woman as an Indigenous woman from the mountains of Guerrero; it's not the same to be a bourgeois white man as an impoverished Black man. And it's important to emphasize all these differences because not all women are oppressed; some of us might experience discrimination and gender violence without being oppressed.

Understanding that there are few oppressions that solely involve "gender" and that speaking of the patriarchy is myopic and inexact, it's clearly neither symbolically nor semantically the same to speak of patriarchy as THE macrostructure as it is to speak of patriarchal relationships that can operate in parallel to other hierarchical relationships without any one of them being THE primary oppression. It's clear that the concept of the matrix of oppressions is broader and more plausible than that of the patriarchy. Nevertheless, the fact that we've never questioned the concept of the patriarchy and we aren't familiar with concepts that are so theoretically refined as the matrix of oppressions or the sex/gender system also has to do with white supremacy.

> When we theorize through white reason, we propose solutions from the perspective of those who have the most and leave behind those who have the least.

As a side note, the matrix of oppressions, patriarchal relationships, and the intersection of oppressions are feminist concepts designed to speak about WOMEN and their differentiated life experiences, and also about racialized men. They aren't there for white men to throw themselves on the ground and cry out *we also suffer*. It's clear that men suffer too, especially if they're situated at the least privileged ends of the matrix of oppressions. And it's essential that we analyze how it's not the same to be a white heterosexual bourgeois man as an impoverished, racialized man and that we make sure not to reproduce systems of oppression when seeking solutions to the problem of sexual hierarchization. But these theories aren't there so the white men who have always been the measure of hierarchies can throw themselves on the ground and cry or discredit feminist demands. Catch up, fuckers.

THE WHITE WOMEN who have monopolized feminist discourse argue that gender is the primordial violence imposed on women's bodies, dictating how they should be. Nevertheless, instead of only taking into account alleged "patriarchal parameters," this concept principally considers their own experiences, which they then use to define womanhood and oppression and femininity. For example, when they discuss how repressed sexuality is one imposition of gender, their standard is white women's sexuality. Not all women receive the same sexual education.

Allow me to suggest an exercise: think of typically feminine qualities, those that have been associated with women or those found when you look up "femininity" or "woman" in the dictionary. The words that come to mind will surely be "sweet" and "fragile" and "tender" and "maternal." These stereotypes are all based on the experiences of white women. This is why the theorist María Lugones argues that "woman"—as an ontological, epistemological, identitarian, and symbolic concept—is white. Women are white. Fragility and repressed sexuality and being confined to private space and goodness are white experiences. Brown women have different forms of socialization and distinct sexualities and varied femininities. Following the tradition of Sojourner Truth, María Lugones makes a distinction between women and females. Women are white; those who are Black and of color are females and they have been bestialized alongside racialized men. Because they are not considered women—as they aren't fragile but sexually powerful and full of rage—they have not been considered in mappings of what it means to be a woman, or in the construction of agendas for liberation.

The problem with the radical theorization of gender lies not only in its emphasis on the experiences of white women, but also in that its reading of these experiences is built on a dichotomy. There are Indigenous women who argue there isn't one single femininity but many, and that not all of them are oppressive: some are emancipatory because they are based on reconnecting with the ancestral. For example, while having long hair is a symbol of oppression for many radicals, for racialized women it means recovering their history, empowerment; it is a vindication, especially when that hair has been used to degrade them. There are racialized feminists who speak of two classes of patriarchal relationships: those articulated around sexual dichotomy are considered high-intensity relationships, while low-intensity relationships are those in which there was/is a sexual duality rather than a dichotomy, and even though community tasks may be divided by sex, this isn't antagonistic or hierarchal. Giving birth and gathering food and raising children were considered to be as valuable as hunting and making war. During colonization processes, something occurs that the Indigenous feminist Julieta Paredes defines as "interlocking patriarchal relationships," which is when sexual hierarchization is imposed on sexual duality. Hence the undervaluation of maternity and care work is consolidated through colonization. Feminists of color thus see abolishing gender as unviable, as we would end up resembling the men who have the most rather than the women who have the least, and this abolition would be a continuation of these colonization processes. They prefer to restore duality so that fertility and care work, tenderness, sexual power, and long/afro hair are resignified and dignified.

FEMINISM WITHOUT A ROOM OF ONE'S OWN

> When we theorize through Eurocentrism,
> we propose racist agendas.

Radical feminism argues that feminism is an internationalism and that what unites us all is that we are women. Which means that instead of there being many feminisms, there's only the one that seeks to liberate women from oppression. Oppression, singular. Which means we don't need white or Indigenous feminism. Verga. I've got nothing to say to these kinds of arguments. It makes me want to kick someone's ass because if there's one thing I can't stand, it's manipulation. Fortunately, Audre Lorde does have something to say: "Being women together was not enough. We were different. Being gay-girls together was not enough. We were different. Being Black together was not enough. We were different. . . . Self-preservation warned some of us that we could not afford to settle for one easy definition."

In the sixties, radical feminism popularized the slogan "Organize around your oppression," calling on women to come together as part of the feminist movement. bell hooks was one of the first women to problematize this slogan. She applauded its call to empathy, but raised a few questions: What is it that oppresses women? Is there a sole oppression? Which is it? Is oppression through sexual hierarchy really the most violent? What does it really mean to be oppressed? bell hooks was emphatic that this political position was the excuse that many privileged women needed to ignore their economic and racial privileges. They were able to deny their privileges under this slogan and there are still radical feminists to this day who argue that women don't have any privileges under patriarchy—perhaps not as women, but as white people and middle- or upper-class people, of course they do. Radical feminists use the premise that all women are oppressed to argue that suffering can't be measured and that women don't have any privileges. Nevertheless, as feminists of color have repeated throughout history, a woman can experience sexist discrimination and still be a racist piece of shit who exploits her domestic workers. Experiencing sexism and being an oppressor at the same time is not an oxymoron, but being white and saying that you're oppressed simply because you're a woman is. You cannot belong to a historically privileged group and then say you're oppressed. Give me a fucking break. To be oppressed, you need to experience at least two systems of oppression and not belong to any historically privileged groups. It's mathematics. It's like an equation. If you're white and a woman and middle class, you experience discrimination and sexism. If you're Black and impoverished, you experience oppression. If you're a woman and impoverished, you experience oppression.

> When we theorize through privilege, we propose solutions that reproduce systems of oppression.

Perhaps women share experiences of sexist discrimination and misogynistic violence and situations of machismo, but differences in class and race separate our lived experiences. There are privileged women and it's not hard to see: privilege isn't about the benefits you take from the system, but how the system automatically benefits you. bell hooks goes further, breaking down the sexual hierarchy and arguing that sexism has never fully determined the lives of all women. She says that being oppressed means lacking options, and many women in this world can choose—no matter how imperfect their choices may be—to access rights that others can't and buy certain freedoms. So, if a woman can make decisions and access rights and buy freedoms, her experiences would be called discrimination or exploitation or sexist violence, but not oppression. bell hooks says it with a brutal honesty. As a Black woman, she belongs to an oppressed (racial) group and experiences sexist discrimination. Her oppression lies not in patriarchal relationships, but in the history of enslavement of people of her race. If you're a white/mestiza/white-passing woman and you're middle or upper class, you're not oppressed because you can choose, you can make decisions, you have access to many rights. Your experience is called sexist discrimination or misogynistic violence. Bitch, please.

> When we theorize through white tears,
> we erase systems of oppression.

Feminism with a room of one's own sees maternity as a step backward, as slavery. And it calls on women to stop reproducing, or to be bad mothers if they do reproduce. Provided, of course, that being a bad mother means leaving your children with an underpaid nanny so you can pursue your career. Radical theorization of maternity is a perfect example of how radical feminism is not just theoretically problematic, but that its biased conclusions have repercussions on the agenda. This feminism, by seeing maternity as a type of oppression, spends too much energy on the issue of abortion; nevertheless, it's not even so important an issue that its decriminalization forms part of a universal agenda. For many women, though, abortion isn't the problem—the problem is forced sterilization. For racialized women, giving birth can be an act of resistance against processes of racial cleansing. Giving birth means perpetuating their guerrilla lineage. Giving birth means going against the establishment that claims we need to better the race. Giving birth means spitting in the face of the racists that want them to be infertile.

> Theorizing through racial privilege
> perpetuates racial extermination.

For radical feminism, the family is an axis of oppression and an institution to be abolished. While racialized feminists have critiqued domestic and intrafamily violence, they also recognize that the family can be a place of refuge from the racism they experience in public space. It also represents the continuity of the community and caring for their family means caring for their race. Care is then a radical defense against the racism that threatens their lives.

> Theorizing through the experience of privilege
> depoliticizes the power of care work
> as resistance to oppression.

Why do we applaud Andrea Dworkin, who is an essayist rather than a theorist, but we don't give the same respect to Angela Davis, who has developed an extraordinary theoretical analysis of the prison–industrial complex? Why do we assume that all women are oppressed if many of us can make decisions, however imperfect they may be? Why don't we listen to bell hooks when she says that not all women are oppressed because being oppressed means not having options? Erasure is also a form of racism.

As we saw over the course of this text, the analyses of women from zulos are theoretically sharper and conceptually more developed. Speaking of the intersection of oppressions is more concrete and brilliant than speaking of the patriarchy.

FEMINISM WITHOUT A ROOM OF ONE'S OWN 93

Speaking of a multiplicity of experiences is closer to reality than speaking of a shared oppression. It's not a coincidence that the most ingenious ideas occur to women from zulos because lived experience, needing to constantly rifártela in the face of racism and precarity, ends up creating more highly developed theoretical processes. The problem with theorizing from a room of one's own not only lies with the fact that it perpetuates the coloniality of knowledge, or with its racist erasure, or with its theoretically unsustainable contributions. The problem is that it forms the basis for solutions. The agenda of feminism with a room of one's own is formulated around privilege, and when it deigns to see other women, it does so through white savior syndrome: *Oh, those poor Nigerian girls, they need international aid in their country to save them from those savage machos!* Or through moralism: *Nothing that makes a man hard is empowering, perreo isn't empowering, no matter what Black women say!* Or through manipulation: *The problem is that whores don't see that selling their snatch affects us all!* Or through personal interest: *We need more women in leadership positions!* Or through the reproduction of racism: *We need to take the hijab away from the Arabs!* Or through classism: *We demand that catcalling by construction workers be punished with prison time!*

When we theorize through race and class privilege,
we propose agendas that reproduce systems
of oppression like racism and classism.

The agenda of feminism with a room of one's own has been hegemonic. The vote. Access to leadership positions. Access to university education. Birth control . . . There are women publishing books. There are women in the army. There are women in the foreign service. There are women in politics. And feminism with a room of one's own has prioritized its agenda and forgotten about the women from zulos. How many feminists go to Black Lives Matter marches? How many protest against the social programs that sterilize Indigenous women? How many demand the abolition of the Aliens Act in Europe? How many support the struggle of traditional midwives, the defense of water and territory, and the Palestinian struggle to keep giving birth as resistance against the occupation? How many denounce the racism of the prohibition of the hijab in public space in Europe? This is why thousands of women from zulos don't see anything liberatory in feminism, because feminism isn't solving their problems. It's time to listen to the voices of women without a room of their own, women who write while sitting on the sidewalk listening to Jenni Rivera and drinking a forty. To the voices of women who defend their land and their right to give birth to children with monolid eyes. It's time to question who cleans up the graffitied walls of our marches and whose shoulders bear the weight of the liberation of those who have the most. To listen to the contributions of racialized feminists and take them seriously. It's time to ask them, *How can I help you?* If we theorize through the matrix of oppressions, different experiences of class and race don't have to separate us. We need a feminist agenda from the zulos. As the Muslim feminist Wadia N Duhni says, "Humanity has failed us, are we going to fail each other too?"

AUTHOR'S NOTE

The introduction to this text is based on the introduction to *King Kong Theory* by Virginie Despentes. I'd like to thank the authors and editors of all the books that formed the theoretical basis of this essay and of my political posture: *Descolonizando*

FEMINISM WITHOUT A ROOM OF ONE'S OWN 95

el feminismo: teorías y prácticas desde los márgenes; Otras inapropiables: feminismo desde las fronteras; This Bridge Called My Back: Writings by Radical Women of Color; Tejiendo de otro modo: feminismo, epistemología y apuestas descoloniales en Abya Yala; The Invention of Women: Making an African Sense of Western Gender Discourses; Feminismos y poscolonialidad: descolonizando el feminismo desde y en América Latina; Feminismos negros, una antología; Feminismo para principiantes; El patriarcado al desnudo: tres feministas materialistas; Devenir perra; Un zulo propio; Malditas; Hilando fino desde el feminismo comunitario; and *Filósofos y mujeres.* I'd also like to make it very clear that, because my context was growing up in a zulo, I didn't understand hegemonic feminism and I didn't know how to verbalize this or theorize the unease and aversion it caused. I didn't have the epistemic tools or the critical apparatus; I only found them when I began to read Black authors and authors of color. So allow me to clearly state that, while my experience is lived because I felt it in my body, the clarity to theorize these experiences and explain my dissent from white feminism in academic terms is thanks to authors and activists such as Angela Davis, María Lugones, Rita Segato, bell hooks, Gloria Anzaldúa, Chela Sandoval, Audre Lorde, Yuderkys Espinosa, Ochy Curiel, Sirin Adlbi Sibai, Wadia N Duhni, Julieta Paredes, Daniela Ortiz, Patricia Hill Collins, Kimberlé Crenshaw, Gayatri Spivak, Valeria Angola, Kerly Garavito, and Jen Rubio.

Alexandra R. DeRuiz
tr. Heather Cleary

PRESERVING TRANS HISTORY

The one duty we owe to history is to rewrite it.

—Oscar Wilde

THE IMPORTANT DOCUMENTATION of the history of transgender, transvestite, and transsexual people is, in my opinion, something that has only recently begun—thanks to the immense work of María Belén Correa with the creation of the Archivo de la Memoria Trans in Argentina, and the publication in Mexico of *Mujercitos*, a doctoral dissertation by Susana Vargas.

Few accounts from people along the trans spectrum have been published in Mexico due to the fact that, for generations, we have been subjected to countless forms of systemic and structural violence in this cis-heteropatriarchal society. We trans survivors are also few: if I'm not mistaken, there are hardly any trans women over seventy years old in Mexico City.

I also know, from personal experience, how hard trans people have fought for the right to be recognized and express ourselves according to the gender we identify as, and how hard it has been to make a place for ourselves in this society that rejects everything considered "abnormal" or "outside the law," as Michel Foucault conceives of the term in *Abnormal*, a collection of his lectures at the Collège de France from 1974 to 1975, in which he describes three categories: the monster, who violates natural laws and social norms; the incorrigible, who is subject to the domestication of the body; and the masturbator. These categories appear in the eighteenth century as a mechanism for disciplining the modern family.

Having said this, I need to state clearly and unconditionally that in my lifetime, from the late '60s through the '70s and '80s, Mexico City was the site of relentless oppression and persecution of everyone who dared to express their identity or to live their sexuality beyond the limits of the normative. For my second book, still in production, *Las vestidas no se olvidan: recuperando la historia trans en la Ciudad de México* (Las Vestidas Will Not Be Forgotten: Recovering Trans History in Mexico City), the greatest challenge has been gathering the stories of trans elders, since most of the trans people of my generation are dead or disappeared, and their stories and testimonies were never shared or written down. I lived in another country for many years—due to persecution and violence, I had to flee my beloved Mexico City, formerly known as El DF, living in Tijuana for a few months before crossing the border as an undocumented immigrant to live in the United States for thirty years. When I returned to Mexico in 2012, I discovered that in all those years, sexual and gender diversity had not been on any political or historical agenda, so I'll start by telling you some of what I remember and what it was like, in my experience, to be trans in Mexico City in the 1970s.

According to my memory, it was around 1975 when I first encountered a group of sexual dissidents. I was working as an assistant to the seamstress for the fashion house Palou at 5 Calle López. One day, I decided to take the metro and walked toward the station along Avenida Juárez. Right on the corner in front of the Palacio de Bellas Artes, there was a fountain where jotas, vestidas, locas, and mariposas[1] would gather. These were the words we used to identify ourselves back then. Of course, there were other slurs that people used to name us. All these girls were sitting around the fountain, just hanging out, and it was a fantastic discovery for my thirteen-year-old self to see so many people like me in the same place—a public place—people who looked like me and didn't care about the people shouting insults at them as they walked by.

I was still in grade school, so I had my uniform on, but I was already wearing lipstick, nail polish, and clogs with wooden heels; I was a hyperfeminine little boy, so when I walked past this group, they noticed me right away, and one of them called out, "Look at the little girl, la chiquilla, la jotita!" And then several others started calling to me, inviting me to come closer. Feeling exposed, I panicked and ran all the way to the metro station. I'll never forget that experience: so many jotas—some wearing makeup and men's clothing, some in dresses and heels, some with short hair, lipstick, and earrings, all of them flamboyant—laughing and calling to me in what seems to me today like a scene out of a surrealist movie.

Months later, I walked through the Zona Rosa for the first time with my childhood friend Karina and a few other vestidas, as we called ourselves. That day, Karina and I were

---

1. Translator's note: These terms will be left in Spanish throughout. "Vestidas" is the feminine plural of "dressed [up]," as in drag; "locas" is the feminine plural of "wild" or "crazy"; "mariposas" means "butterflies." "Jotas" is the feminine plural form of "joto," a slur derived from the "J" (pronounced "jota") wing where gay men were jailed in Mexico City's infamous Lecumberri Prison, which was operational from 1900 to 1977.

in the Glorieta de Insurgentes, a sunken plaza connected to the metro station bearing its name. In the mid-1970s, urban tribes would gather there, heterosexuals mingling with people we know today as LGBT, regardless of social class, some in groups and some seated on the ring of concrete that encircled the space. Some would sit in chairs at the cafés and restaurants that existed in the plaza, turning the area into a meeting point for all kinds of activities. On this occasion, Karina and I were with a group of vestidas: La Georgette, La Claudio, La María Félix, Enrique La Galleta, and La Princesa Mérit, who was a minor like Karina and me, but she was already a vestida; that is, she was already transfeminine, which was admirable back then.

At thirteen, I was awestruck by the experience, by seeing so many vestidas together, queering around and talking about countless things I didn't understand yet. I remember that's where I met Miss Dior, Miss Clairol, La Licuadora, La Viuda, Katia, and so many other vestidas, some of whom were very femme, others who were already on hormones, and others who were more masculine, like La Licuadora, the blender, whose real name I never knew. These were times of terrifying violence against people like me, like us, people who dared to challenge what we now call heteronormativity and the gender binary, to challenge the categories of masculine and feminine.

In my case, I identify as a transfeminine person, and it's important for me to mention other people who dared to challenge the gender binary in my time, people who paved the way for future generations; we owe them recognition because they managed to shift the way society viewed nonconforming people in that era. In my long trajectory, I have met so many wonderful people who have not only challenged society in one way or another but have also stood up to the system and transgressed the norms imposed on us. My contribution to the anthology *México se escribe con J: una historia de la cultura gay* (Mexiqueer: A History of Gay Culture in Mexico) is an essay titled "Jotas, vestidas, cuinas, locas y mariposas: Historias del movimiento trans en la Ciudad de México" (Jotas, Vestidas, Queens, Locas and Mariposas: Histories of the Trans Movement in Mexico City), in which I describe my experience and talk about the figures who had an impact on my life, like Xóchitl and her princesses, whom I mention in the context of one of the parties Xóchitl organized in luxury hotels and resorts outside the city. Here is a paragraph from that essay, where I talk about the importance of not forgetting them:

> There were too many important people at the party to count. Marta Valdez-Pinos was there; she was the owner of several colorful watering holes like DeVal, an iconic nightclub back in those days. Also in attendance was Guillermo Ocaña, better known as Camelia la Tejana; a respected event promoter and agent, rumor has it that he was also one of the founders of the famous and elitist bar El 9. Camelia la Tejana acted as the master of ceremonies that night. Mitzy Gay, who had just recently won the Miss Gay pageant, was there, too; he was just starting to make a name for himself in the world of celebrity fashion, but he would go on to become a famous designer in Mexico and the United States and dress stars like Verónica Castro, María Félix, and many more. That night, the show was courtesy of Francis, whose drag career was on the rise, with help from Xóchitl, of course; over the years, Francis would become an international

star. Also present, naturally, was Naná, known as the Queen of the Zona Rosa for her beauty and for being one of the few trans women in those days for whom doors would be opened and traffic would literally stop.

Xóchitl, or Gustavo Ortega Maldonado, as her inner circle knew her, was a mystical person who remains shrouded in myth and all kinds of stories, some of which might be true and others made up. What is indisputable, though, is that those of us who had the chance to be in the presence of Xóchitl—queen, mother, and lady; the one and only—will never forget her or the impact she had not only on LGBT communities but on everyone around her, including celebrities like film and television stars, writers, politicians, designers, promoters, and so on, as well as society in general. Xóchitl wasn't just someone with power who could pull strings with people in different social spheres—she was also someone who challenged society with the way she presented herself in public and who used her power so others, including many trans people, could get ahead. It's a fact that many people found success in different fields back then because of their connection to Xóchitl. I can't think of another icon who had as profound an impact on my life and the lives of the people I knew, regardless of class, stigmas, or stereotypes. Xóchitl wasn't just an entrepreneur who managed brothels and organized events, who knew people in politics and the arts and had a way of opening doors for nonconforming people so we could have a place in society, she was also a support system for many in my inner circle, like Naná and Raquel. Xóchitl encouraged them and supported their development and productivity; she made space for them, taking them under her wing like her daughters. For me, Xóchitl wasn't only the

Queen of all Queens, she was also the Mother to all vestidas in those days.

In Mexico City, my beloved ex-DF, there have always been social justice movements; groups have always organized to express their discontent and protest against corrupt, oppressive governments. We cannot forget the student movement in 1968 and the massacre at Tlatelolco, the 1971 Halconazo that murdered and disappeared so many young people, or, more recently, the forced disappearance of forty-three students from Ayotzinapa. All of these were crimes committed by the state.

It was in 1978, on the tenth anniversary of the Tlatelolco massacre, that a contingent including gay, lesbian, bisexual, and trans people joined the march to give visibility to their struggle and express their rage against the system that oppressed, persecuted, and criminalized them for the simple fact of their sexual orientation, identity, or gender expression. In the prologue to *Voces del Otro Lado* (Voices from the Other Side), the professor and my esteemed colleague Ernesto Reséndiz Oikión recounts this historic event and the movement it sparked, reminding us that when the Homosexual Front for Revolutionary Action (FHAR), the Lambda Group for Homosexual Liberation, and the autonomous group Oikabeth took to the streets demanding sexual liberation, their action catalyzed the creation of publications that later helped share information about these organizations.

The following year, in June of 1979, these groups got organized, and they organized the first LGBT march in Mexico City to call for an end to police harassment and extortion, and to demand that our rights as citizens be respected. I remember joining the march, which began at the Monumento a los Niños Héroes in Chapultepec and ended at the Alameda, right in front of Bellas Artes, if memory serves. It was the first time that we trans women—nosoTRANS—dared to walk the city streets, many of us in heels and long dresses, others in boots and miniskirts. I remember wearing a halter top and shorts with high-heeled sandals and will certainly never forget the insults hurled at us, the cries of "jotos," "maricones," "putos," and "degenerados," among so many others. At one point, they started throwing things at us, garbage, I think, even fruit and other waste. I will always remember that moment of community empowerment, when we saw that we were, in fact, able to resist and challenge an oppressive system that criminalized and harassed us.

A few years ago, I assisted Dr. Kris Klein Hernández, a historian and professor at a university in the United States, with a research project about a doctor who practiced sex reassignment surgeries, or gender-affirming surgeries, in Mexico in the 1950s. Supposedly, the first trans person to undergo this surgery was Marta Olmos, and it was performed by Dr. Rafael Sandoval Camacho. In the research process, we discovered that Dr. Siobhan Guerrero Mc Manus wrote in 2014 about this doctor and the surgeries he performed in the state of Veracruz.

We tried to find a case that preceded Marta Olmos's, even searching social media and talking with trans elders in Veracruz, but found nothing beyond the writings of Drs. Sandoval Camacho and Guerrero Mc Manus. Recently, we uncovered another article published in 2023 in which Professor Ryan M. Jones from SUNY Geneseo confirms that, in 1954, Marta Olmos became the first trans person in Mexico to undergo what today is known as gender confirmation surgery.

It was toward the end of 2017 when I felt the need to recover and preserve the history and memoirs of my trans siblings, but unfortunately, this has been a challenge, since—given my exile in the United States, the HIV/AIDS pandemic, and the fact that most trans people of my generation have either died or disappeared—there are virtually no history or testimonial accounts told by trans people of earlier generations.

The system's repression of LGBT people from the 1960s through the '80s has not been adequately documented or made visible. Nor is there an official archive to legally document all the injustices committed against trans people in those days. This is why I feel an obligation and a responsibility to not only visibilize but also recover and vindicate the struggles of the LGBT movement, no matter how difficult.

Decades have passed, and the testimonies of trans survivors still have not been gathered within a legal framework in order to foster historic reparations. It is essential that these stories be told, that new generations learn that the long path to our civil and human rights was paved with the blood and suffering of our ancestors who fought for our right to express ourselves and to be trans, to resist oppression as trans people, and to love ourselves and each other as trans people.

Lia García, La Novia Sirena (The Mermaid Bride)
tr. Gabriela Ramirez-Chavez

TO SEA CHANGE:
METAPHORS OF TRANS' PAIN

I AM A water woman, that is what my ancestors say. Daughter of Oshún, the mother of all rivers that run, flow, and die as they become the sea, water—Yemayá. The water is my refuge from all my sorrow and rage because in it I feel free; everything flows in it, the way it does within my body and my gender. Everything is transparent like my sisters and I who face the world each day despite being insulted and ridiculed for breaking out of the norms imposed by colonial patriarchy. Sometimes, the water is cloudy like the tornado I feel when they make me feel that I don't belong, that the world is not for bodies like mine, that with each step I risk never making it back home. Water gives me everything. When I let my body float, I feel nature embracing all the wounds this body carries, this body that has survived violent colonization and a crushing patriarchy. As I float, I realize I'm slowly turning into a mermaid, because I can dive and explore new rhythms of moving in water. I can swim against the tide, feel cold and warm currents, and above all, face big waves that have taught me how, in order to move past them, you have to dive deep or swim toward them. The water has been my home since I was a little girl. In it, I learned to look at my whole body and embrace it with tenderness, I learned to bare myself, to let myself fall, to discover the world below, where the roots are. And above all, I learned to not fear the abyss no matter how dark it is because to be an abyss, you must swallow light.

To think of the sea is also to think of all the mermaids the sea has taken so they could make the depths their home. They say to sink is to grow deep, and writing this story in the first person with all the radical tenderness sown in my tongue takes me into the deep, where I meet the mermaids, smile at them, touch their hair, feel their skin again, and tell them that here, in the world, we have not forgotten them, that we're doing everything we can to take care of their chosen families, to keep their faces on our altars, to say their names every morning before going out into the world weighed down by the possibility that it might be our last day, but feeling whole because we know if this happens, the mermaids will receive us in their depths.

When I go down to the depths, I want to tell them that their names are the seeds of our rage, of our trans'[1] fury, of the collective memory that others try to wrest from us when we shout for "Life, Memory, and Justice!" in the streets, in schools, in markets, in the corners of hotels, on busy streets, on public transportation, in the ears of those who, despite seeing us, do not listen. There I, you, we are present, in the echo of our lived experience.

---

1. The apostrophe after the word trans' refers to our many experiences with identities in transit/transmutation, which live within trans' people. It is an affective way to embrace, in writing, all our experiences and gender expressions, which are fluid, and not reduce them to rigid categories that move only from one point to another. The apostrophe represents the wind, movement, and communication in our ancestral codexes, where trans' people exist. The trans experience is trans' because it opens a world of fragmented possibilities to inhabit the body, gender, sexuality, and spirituality.

I am the woman who writes, and I invite you who embrace these words to call me by whatever name you choose: the name that most reminds you of a sister the sea took into the deep or, maybe, all the names that you wished were yours as a girl, boy, or nonbinary child. Say those names and they will surely manifest themselves here, at home, in bed, on the bus, at the park, or wherever you hold my words. Whisper the name you have for me, and it will fill me with tenderness. Because what would become of this world without the possibility of transiting over and over like a snake that sheds, leaving a trace of what it once was and became again, despite all the pain this process entails and with all the wisdom of turning poison into an antidote? What would become of this world without us mermaids who, to become mermaids, had to learn to transform our pain into strength, our most precious possession, which we now embrace to keep moving forward?

ANOTHER OF THE most valuable things the sea taught me was to remember the wisdom of my grandmother Virginia. As a young woman, she searched for pearls on the shores of Puerto Ángel, a place where rocks embrace the waves' final moment. There, she would find mollusks with black, scratchy shells hiding among the rocks so no one could uncover their truth—the truth of those slow, rocky shoreline creatures who had taken years to reach the place where sand and water meet, to sunbathe for a few days before returning to deep waters, where they would celebrate having survived their transit. Those creatures, my grandmother would tell me, held the greatest secret that every mermaid should know: the pearls they birthed were the product of their pain. I remember the first time my grandmother told my brother and me this story, she pulled out of her drawer a box containing fifteen shiny pearls of all shapes and sizes. My mom used to leave us at our grandmother's house for a few days whenever she had to work in another village. My grandmother would lay us on her big bed and light a candle to put us to sleep. For her, light is what guided us to our dreams. That first time, she told us her mother had given her those pearls and that, like her grandmother, all the women in the family kept pearls because they had learned to turn their pain into their most valued treasure. That was a very difficult moment for me because, at only six years of age, I was still a prisoner to the masculinity being imposed on me and I felt a deep pain inside knowing that pearls were never going to be for me, although everything suddenly changed when I grew up and decided to embrace the pearls of my ancestors.

"Pearls, my little ones, are not a matter of elegance. Pearls contain a mystery that can only be revealed to those who have learned to see life with eyes full of water, like the women in our family. For a pearl to be born from the mollusk that holds it, ten years must pass. That's about how long it takes to coat the bacteria that has torn its fragile spongy interior. It encapsulates the bacteria in nacre to make its wound a pearl, and another pearl and another."

Can you imagine what it feels like to open a mollusk and find the memory of its wounds turned into precious, shiny pearls? Smooth pearls that don't damage but rather embrace its interior. At the same time, these pearls put the mollusk at risk because of this world's hunger to profit from them, from their wounds. To steal their pain, their scars, and sell them to the jewelry industry, which displays on white necks the history of our pain incarnate. Oh Grandma, those pearls of yours taught us so much! Small yet endowed with great strength, as great as the cry of our trans' resistance. I write this story with a long pearl necklace hanging from my neck, embracing the Adam's apple that remains and reminds me of the boy I once was, and even of my father and my grandparents who, despite being hard on me and denying me their love when I decided to say goodbye to generational masculinity, are still with me. These pearls result from my pain. From everything I do with the living memory of my wounds and my scars: "Here, it hurt. Here, it healed. And here it will be transformed." These pearls belong to me, I reclaim them from the patriarchal and misogynistic cis-tem that tries to steal our painful stories and erase the archive of our pain; that tries to sell our pain to their finest tabloids, which put our dismembered, tortured, and mutilated bodies on display without even acknowledging our feminine identities, turning us instead back into what the state has always wanted us to be under its masculine domination. These pearls are a cry of truth that speak to my feminine disobedience, to my trans'cestry, which connects me to all the women who always embraced me with their gazes, ready to receive me when I decided to become a mermaid, those women who saw my feminine birth in the water, from the water, and for the water, longing for the beauty of ambiguity and this deep, commanding voice that guides and remembers, one by one, all the lives of all the mermaids who rest under the clarity that brought me back to this certainty: my existence is resistance, and the woman I am exists because one night, face covered in tears, she looked in the mirror and stopped fearing her own self. I shout her name, I will never again let go of that girl who was born among pearls, songs of water, and justice woven to the rhythm of a *son*.

They say humans have only explored 20 percent of the world's waters, and that they dominate only 30 percent of these with the abilities they possess as a rational species. Saying this takes me back to my grandmother's bedtime stories in her room, which my brother and I always thought smelled like "grandma." We could never describe that smell, but it was like wood combined with roses and old books. We loved that smell, so characteristic of my grandmother; it comes to us from time to time when we go back to our hometown and she manifests herself. We know she takes care of us when we go for a swim or are about to go to sleep. My grandmother never told us scary stories, she only told us the lore of her town, like the story of the women who gathered pearl mollusks at night, moving them into deep waters with their brothers' and husbands' boats, freeing them so no one would find and steal their pearls. Those land and water mermaid-women deftly swam the flowing waters to release that pain, to make it reach the bottom of the blue ocean, which holds the memory of all my sisters found in the water. Because in this country, the waters also keep the memory of disappeared women, of their nameless bodies, of the souls that float despite their aggressors' attempts to hide the evidence. These women knew that at the bottom of that striking sea they were among many missing bodies that the town still searched for on land, while their echoing voices shouted their true whereabouts.

THIS COUNTRY WHERE I live—my land, my water, Mexico— is a country at war with trans' women. Every day I shed ocean-tears when I learn the names of my sisters murdered in a place taken over by machismo and transphobic hatred, which lurk in our spaces and take our lives, dreams, futures, and memories. Despite this, we have not lost any of these women, we have found them: their voices still resound in our skin, the largest and most visible organ-territory of our bodies, and in our caresses . . . and in our desire-turned-water to shout the counter-history of all women who say YES, they *were* able to stop the hands of their aggressors and run away without looking back to continue their path and become names, each a name that is named . . . Alessa, Itzel, Valeria, Cheva, Paola, Gloria, Itzayana, Elizabeth, Patricia, María, Jaqueline, Teresa, Malena, and so many others, her and her and her, and them, all of us . . . TOGETHER.

We talk about and for these women so much. In this country, talking about my sisters murdered by transphobia is an act of resistance that makes visible our painful memory and demands justice and reparation. While some sisters in this city are fighting so all dissident bodies can have human rights, freedom of expression, their identities recognized, and access to quality medical care, other sisters are infiltrating the cultural realm, where no matter how many human rights have been established, sexist, racist, misogynist, and transphobic violence still exists. The violence that claims women's lives in this country is committed by men who have been raised under an oppressive model, with an atrocious thirst for power and the multifarious annihilation of our bodies. Thirteen women are murdered every day; of these women, four are brown-skinned trans' women engaged in sex work. Four lives stripped of the possibility of dreaming, imagining, and weaving memories in their communities, lands, and home, and I keep wondering: How many men? How many men are fugitives with blood-stained hands and mouths full of guilt and the saliva of my sisters, the ones searched for by Rocío, Alejandra, and me—along with you, who are reading my words—and all the other women searching for those pearls to release them into the deep? How many men are controlled by the patriarchy and exterminate us who live in feminine resistance? How many men preach hate, abuse, rape, mutilation, disappearance? How many men silence our mouths, the truth sown

to sink is to grow deep

in our tongues? How many men carry the stories of women they've denied the right to see their mothers, their mirrors, their teddy bears, their lipsticks and wigs again—all those women with a firm, tender desire to change, to change and transmute. How many children are blinded by their parents and forced to stand before a bridge of imposed masculinity? How many men are imprisoned by a buried desire they prefer to exchange for deaths, taking the lives of my sisters, yours, and ours?

I ask myself these questions every day when my sisters share the news with us of yet another transfemicide here in the city, in another state of the republic, or in Oaxaca, my grandmother's land. Even in Puerto Ángel on the Costa Chica of the Pacific, where three of my aunts live, married to boatmen who embark on long journeys to put food on the table and sell their catch to survive. Going back to the pier is always healing for me, because it reunites me with the water and those depths that hide so much memory.

My life in Mexico City as an Afro-descendant trans' woman is difficult because the violence I face due to my gender identity is compounded by daily racism. Going to college has allowed me to make my resistance visible in an academic space that has historically talked about us, without us—where we have needed to navigate colonial extractivism as dirty as polluted waters made murky by a lack of care and affection for the living territory where our bodies are born and grow, far from the city.

One of my most personal and poetic interests when I began my undergraduate studies in education was the subject of my voice. When I turned fifteen, my voice began to change, it grew deeper, very similar to that of my father and my brother, and although it was strange and painful because I did not like that sudden change, I lacked the tools to do anything about it. My voice is my home, but in order to make it my home, I had to embrace it. It is a very deep voice and when it comes out in daily interactions, people look at me with confusion or morbid fascination, whisper among themselves, and even refer to me with masculine pronouns although my appearance says the complete opposite. It is a moment of simultaneity between political unveiling and the risk of becoming visible: because I am seen as what I want people to see—a trans' woman, an ambiguous body, a woman with a deep voice who escapes the normative—but I should tell you, this is also very dangerous because of what could happen. The male gaze is confrontational: constantly dealing with that gaze exhausts us, drains our energy, makes us feel stripped of our bodies.

I remember my colleague Agnes Torres (a trans' comrade murdered in Puebla in 2012), by quoting her: "Discrimination begins in the mouth." I think, though, that it begins in the gaze, and I'm sure you would agree how hard and exhausting it is to deal with the masculine energy overflowing this city. We trans' women are haunted by stories of violent encounters when we think of the masculinity that desires us (desires the forbidden) silently and secretly, and at the same time uses us as a metaphor for their own forbidden desire in order to annihilate it. What do men kill about themselves in the act of killing us? Why us?

IN PUERTO ÁNGEL, Oaxaca, where my aunts Elida, Martha, and Concepción live, there is a seafood restaurant called La Doña Luna. It is a place on the coast that serves tourists from many countries who visit the town year after year to eat fresh-caught fish. There, my aunt Elida's friend Dina has three photographs of three boatmen who were once well known in the town. She says that one night they went fishing and never returned because they were taken by a mermaid. A nameless mermaid enchanted them with her forbidden song and drowned them in a deep sleep. Only the empty boat was found, capsized and without a trace of the men. They had drowned.

Everyone on the town's ageless pier knows that if a fisherman goes to sea and does not return, it's because he heard the voice of the mermaid that hides in the depths and comes out on dark foggy nights to sing with her enchanting voice, making fishermen lose their minds and arrive at the conclusion "I feel, therefore I am." Then they embrace her and dive deep, never to resurface. How brave of those men who decide to listen to the mermaid song and trans'form themselves into something far removed from the masculinity they were told was "normal." No one is normal when they stop being normal.

Danger, seduction, and desire run through us mermaids. We are water creatures, mysterious deities, women with deep voices who enchant and make you transit between life and death. I think a lot about my fisherman uncles still in Puerto Ángel—there, near the water—who were born and raised a few yards from the sea, and I wonder, as I sit here in Mexico City, forced into lockdown by the state during a pandemic:

What do these water men tell us about being men?

What relationship do they have with the sea?

Might their patriarchal pacts dissolve more easily because they live near water?

Inevitably, I remember myself as a girl living in the body of a sad and confused boy, swimming in the river near my grandmother's house, which was close enough to the sea to have a slight taste of salt. I remember my grandfather and neighbors seeing me happy and saying, yes, I was just like a little shark. "More like a mermaid," my grandmother would say, and they would just laugh, but nodding their heads. My uncles' voices are still with me, and I remember being that shark under the water, shedding its skin to emerge as a mermaid. The men I grew up with were somewhat different because they were connected to the water and the land. Even with their machismo, even as prisoners of a conservatism more intense than that of the city, since they lacked access to new information that would allow them to even ask the question *Who are men?* They were not educated in a way that would allow them to discuss their experiences as men close to the sea. Still, something connects them to this mysterious, feminine, and imposing sea: other times, other tides, and other desires, which I have always tried to reveal through my voice, which is connected to theirs.

My pedagogy of radical tenderness has always been affective and liberating. It makes possible the escape from discipline and sparks critical approaches in which my body and my experience serve as a bridge that connects to the trans' experience in ways that are not conceptual or rational, but rooted in ritual, image, horizontal dialogue, and are always life affirming, because my voice is the center of my existence.

FOR A LONG time, I have worked closely on, and with, masculinity to understand myself as a trans' woman who experienced its imposition in a situated way, and to make men aware, to make them do the work and assume responsibility as principal actors in this context of death and pain. What sustains me today are my feminine roots, my feminine ancestors, my shamans—friends and teachers—my neighbors, and the living memory of those who inhabit the deep. I feel a strong desire to return to my masculine roots and dissolve the patriarchal pacts that oppress this deep way of being, as the deep-voiced trans' mermaid who decided to sing for the boatmen of Puerto Ángel to show them another possible world, another possible way of relating to the experience of trans' women that is more affectionate, warm, and in touch with our needs. I want to be the mermaid who emerges from the deep to trans'form violence into resilience and name my pearl sisters who live on in the abyss. I want to hear the experiences of men close to the sea, to build a bridge between them and the experiences I hear from men who live in the city.

All these questions make me feel like those women who searched for hidden pearls to carry and release into the open sea. All these questions connect me to my male ancestors in a new way that can trans'form my environment while leaving traces on the water so we can continue this arduous, utopian but necessary journey of talking about aggressors, their violence, their experiences, and the roots of their desire to annihilate.

I imagine an intimate learning space on the shore, a space of listening freely and without fear to the voice of the mermaid who invites you to lose all reason and feel again. A mermaid who wishes to heal the colonial wound of masculinity with radical tenderness, softness, and hope; a brave mermaid who has learned to face the eyes of the aggressor and see behind him the full weight of history. A mermaid who, despite being a mermaid, still fears the sea. A mermaid convinced that one day all the bullets they fired will be taken back. A mermaid who knows, from my ancestors, that on a full moon one day, all my sisters the sea has taken will emerge to shed their tears upon the

··· Some things can only be seen by eyes That have cried

earth, to water the new future we all envision and hope for with every beat of our hearts. That mermaid has a name. It is mine. The one I chose for myself the night I was born, giving birth to myself among the fish, birdsong announcing my existence.

Jimena González
tr. Gabriela Jauregui

THE OTHERS

The women in my family
on my father's side
are always "the others."
They have no name
when they're called
by their so-called
lovers.

All Josephines
crying purple stains
hidden on their necks.

All Josephines
waiting
for Benito to
quit his marriage
quit drinking
quit living.

On the side of Luz
my roots are women
decorated with "de"—
desperate women,

despised, degraded, dejected
but always always
always devoted.

I write
to heal myself, to heal them,
to be more than victims,
someone rather than "something,"
so much more than "others."

To unlearn the competition
they instilled in us

I write to learn
that we love lots and many
and we shouldn't feel ashamed.

That we desire many,
we desire them lots.
And that should never hurt.

Because I come from a family
of women who feel forced
to laugh at the offensive jokes
of their drunken husbands.

Of shut-in shut-up women—
I write to teach them to scream, to rip the
you-shut-ups
from their souls.

THE OTHERS 129

I write for my grandmother Josephine,
may she be reborn as a dancer.

For my aunt, may she never cry.
May her bones never hurt again.

For my grandmother María, may she leave
my grandfather many more times.
May she have many boyfriends,
many, many times more
and may she keep writing poetry
and not be afraid
to show her breasts.

I cry out for the bloody knees
of my great-grandmother Emilia,
fulfilling her vows to the Virgin.
May she be reborn
on the coast of Guerrero
and tear down the altars like a tsunami.

I wrap their roots around my feet
and their clouds around my hands.
So that Ale may never return to Morelos
and Gabriela may soon tire of Noé.
So that pain may leave us
with the same ease
our fathers left.

So that I may never again see
my eleven-year-old body
sprawled across the kitchen floor
begging for forgiveness.

So that I never again have to feed
my grandfather
and his lascivious eyes.

And so that I never again need to defend
the purity
of false prophet blood relatives
who squeezed my breast
till I broke.

So that no bastard
rubs his body ever again
on my cousin's legs
on her way back from school.

May we break the damned
damned vicious circle
of "family secrets"
stained with child abuse,
incest, blows, and blood.

So that we may all
be named.

So this will
thunder on
and on in our heads
until we scream.

I lift my voice to recognize
that we have a name,
And that we won't let them forget it.

Gabriela Jauregui
tr. Julianna Neuhouser

DISOBEDIENT TOOLS

"Writing the body," as Woolf asked
and Hélène Cixous asks, is only the beginning.
We have to rewrite the world.

—Ursula K. Le Guin,
"The Fisherwoman's Daughter"

HOW DO WE rewrite the world when "the master's tools will never dismantle the master's house," as the great poet Audre Lorde declared in 1979 at the first National March on Washington for Lesbian and Gay Rights? I've always connected with this idea: neither racism nor the patriarchy can be ended from within. I have never believed institutional critique from within the institution itself to be terribly effective, which is why I'm not part of the academy. But then I ask myself: So where do we begin? Along what line of flight, in which philosophical vestibule must we position ourselves to escape from our current state of death? What tools must we use? As women—beyond merely being or defining ourselves as women—which tools are ours, ones we can use to build a world in which we are safe, where we can thrive rather than survive? How can we speak from a place that does not replicate what we criticize, that does not become cissexist, classist, or racist, idealizing certain types of bodies at the expense of other, different ones? How can we broaden our thinking? How can we become hospitable? We have invented new tools of our own, and we have also resisted by using others that have been détourned. Who has access to them? To whom have we ceded them and from whom have we taken them (sometimes, yes, even by force)? From where do they emerge, what asymmetries do they (re)produce, and who bears this burden?

Language is one of these tools; among our most ancient technologies, it is one we constantly struggle to transform, readapting and reimagining it on a daily basis. If practically everything is mediated by language, then how should we seek another way of telling, as John Berger would say—one that doesn't gloss over, knock down, push aside, leave out? A difficult task yet a necessary one, not one that seeks unquestioning consensus but rather heterogeneity.

So we must make our point of departure in/from heterogeneity: we depart, we take part, we are partial in difference. We speak and write in this tongue that is a legacy of colonialism, the same one with which they have tried to silence us in so many ways for centuries. And yet this is precisely where strength can be found: in the shared word, that fabric we cast like a net in which we are intertwined and entangled. We're entangled, then. We're committed. Consummated. Obstinately continuing. Ursula K. Le Guin asks, in the text that provided the epigraph, *The Fisherwoman's Daughter*, "Where does a woman write, what does she look like writing, what is my image, your image, of a woman writing?"

So, let's stop for a minute. What do you see?

Many times before, and in many ways, I've denounced—most concretely, I feel, in a project for eight hands called *Taller de Taquimecanografía* (Typing Workshop)—the obligatory response: that a woman writing is taking dictation. I've also had to reply, because the circumstances don't allow for anything else, that a woman writing is a dead woman. Silenced. Dismembered. In the trunk of a car. But I have not come here today to speak of those endings. I have come to imagine beginnings, to depart, to think of fissures, to disaffirm (myself), to

DISOBEDIENT TOOLS

ask (myself) questions, writing with precision. These are my tools. How can I free them from the master's clutches? How can we *hack* language so that it becomes ours? How can we readapt it? How can we describe our insubordination?

We can find many examples in the history of feminism, from the most contemporary queer and transfeminist applications of hormones (see the extremely interesting experiments by Paul Preciado narrated in *Testo Junkie*) to the seventies practice of using a speculum as a tool for self-knowledge and self-care, to name a few. But there were already ways of communicating, of making the commons—which will never be, nor should they be, universal. The most powerful acts of resistance can be found in communities where women are largely those responsible for defending the territory, searching for the disappeared, and preserving their language, putting their bodies and knowledge on the line. There are also older methods of communicating resistance: here I think of that woman who stitched encrypted messages into the designs of her quilts along the Underground Railroad, or those from countries in the Middle and Far East who weave rugs with messages in their knots to this day. I think of those housewives and single mothers who came together at Tupperware parties to put "a little something" aside or make a living, but also—and perhaps most importantly—to flee from those kitchens that were often prisons, flee to tell their tales of domestic violence, of clandestine abortions, of survival, something that still occurs under the patriarch's nose through catalog sales and the practice known in Mexico as tandas,[1] or in the tortilla line among immigrant communities in the US (a site

---

1.Translator's note: A tanda is a rotating savings and credit association in which each member makes a periodic contribution, which one member will receive in full each period, allowing people (mostly women) without access to formal credit to make large purchases.

of organizing for Latino Health Access in southern California, for example).[2] Another example more directly connected to the question of how women write today—the most mundane, everyday answer, but one that crosses race and class lines and national borders—is on their cell phones, on social media, and in group chats for people who identify as women or nonbinary.[3] It's obviously important to mention that these spaces are in constant friction with their technological platforms because those tools are created by the purest capitalism and the most absolute market ideology and are therefore not the best arenas for mobilization. I don't even know if I should call them safe spaces, as they're under surveillance to a certain extent, but they're still spaces for free expression, spaces of diversity. A first step, perhaps. Because despite their problems—yes, despite them—something's happening there, in the most visible and the most hidden spaces of the web. So, how shall we reuse or, in the words of Nadia Cortés, rewrite those tools of capital? How do we détourn them? First of all, if we think of them as

2. More recently, a number of women (most of them mothers) in the United States created what appeared to be innocuous "suburban mom" WhatsApp groups and GoFundMe pages to help pay bonds, organize caravans, and volunteer to transport immigrants in detention centers from one side of the country to the other to be reunited with family members waiting for them. For example, see https://www.azcentral.com/story/news/politics/immigration/2018/07/06/moms-help-immigrant-mom-yeni-gonzalez-reunite-separated-children-zero-tolerance-eloy-nyc/758502002/.

3. Or, as Dahlia de la Cerda writes elsewhere in this book, "I wrote it in the dead time of my office job and while doing the laundry. I wrote it in my kitchen and on the steps down to the patio. I wrote it on the toilet and I wrote it as tears ran down my face and I wrote it because my psychiatrist told me that hitting people wasn't a good way of expressing my rage. I wrote it at my stall at the tianguis where I spent years selling used clothes in order to make it to the end of the month. I also wrote it on the Number 2 bus on my way to the mental hospital."

spaces that are diverse, divergent, détourned, then our politics are already transfeminine; in these space-times, as Raquel Gutiérrez observes in her essay in *Más allá del feminismo: caminos para andar*, "a specific language is produced that time and again insists on speaking, that persistently attempts to communicate. And here it's worth reiterating that I'm not referring to any sort of essentialism. We are all women in such different ways that sometimes we don't even recognize each other." And here I would once again invoke those whose gender escapes the binary or cissexist definitions of *woman* or *the feminine* in their most closed, conservative sense, particularly the limited definitions made by certain groups of women and through which they have defined their "feminism." That definition had already been expanded by the bodies of those who came before me, and it is that definition I make use of here. Rather than expand the "universal" (that is, the neutral, man as humanity degree zero) in order to be included, we should instead think of how we have already expanded our own definition, our enunciation, of gender to become so much more. Here is a note that refuses to be consigned to the margins, that interrogates us from below, leaping up from the footer: here and in the rest of the text, I disappropriate the word *woman* to refer to any person who identifies as such, beyond just those who are cis and/or heterosexual, as it is a word used by many trans and nonbinary people to name themselves and I feel that many of the same questions and forms of violence affect all our lives, all our bodies. This also applies to my use of the word *feminine* in this text. Let's use these words as safe conducts in the hope that we'll keep transforming our language to produce a vocabulary that's better adapted to our realities. This doesn't come from a false desire to be "correct," as I am disinterested in correctness and I advocate for disobedience and complexity, but, as Helen

Hester argues in *Xenofeminism*, "the aim of this proliferation is not the beautiful blooming of a hundred drop-down menu options, but the stripping away of social ramifications associated with the heterosexual matrix." We must search.

Yet I wonder, yes, and always wandering, I become entangled. I come here, then, to speak of voices, to articulate a horizon of words woven in virtual spaces—not spaces of an alternative modernity, but rather, as Márgara Millán says, an alternative to modernity. Hacked spaces, spaces that slowly open up under the eye of our very master, capital, patriarchy, the state, blinding it to what is being woven here: a profuse, diffuse fabric in which we seek out other kinds of relationships. In the many groups in which I participate, there are women and nonbinary people speaking and creating languages specific to these spaces. There are people hearing each other out, respecting their shared diversity and even agreeing to disagree, making use of one of the most important political gestures: listening. We're faced with the sensation, as Raquel Gutiérrez has described it, that living under an "existing sex/gender [system] is like being asked ... to translate from our 'mother tongue,' from our patterns of understanding." Faced with perpetual translation, let's open up spaces for active listening. For a lingua franca. For frankness. Here, although some may be quiet, none are silenced. An antiauthoritarian space opens up.

One question comes to mind: How can we maintain virtual spaces as spaces of subversion, whether in spite of technology or because of it? How can we avoid falling into the traps of capitalist conservatism and oppressive despair that characterize online activities? How can we undermine the fact that these tools are only crutches (and how can we use these crutches to strike back at patriarchy)? How can we use them as nonmonopolized sources of knowledge? How can we keep ourselves from exercising power over a distance in a space without bodies? Likewise, how can we declare this space to be one of pleasure and delight? While the differences among us could reconstitute dynamics of marginalization or subalternization, even neocolonialism when they go unmarked and thus "unseen" (skin color, body shape, etc.), how can we make them liberatory in these spaces? How can we ensure that the absence of our bodies does not erase difference in search of an easy, "comfortable" anonymity? The body is one of the sites that rightfully calls into question the diffuse and ethereal nature of these spaces: to me, one of the most interesting, politically relevant aspects of virtual spaces for women and nonbinary people is precisely that, if our bodies have been repositories of sexist, classist, racist violence—I hear myself arguing for the first time in favor of mediation between bodies and I'm surprised and I contradict myself, as all my previous texts and explorations were aimed at a situated politics of a highly present body, such as at parties—then these virtual spaces, where bodies are wrapped in layers, allow them to become less essential or essentialized. It's not that they're dematerialized, but that other ways of feeling and making the body arise in their place. In spaces where bodies come wrapped in layers and layers, possibilities suddenly emerge to speak of things that would otherwise go unspoken, to feel at peace with silence in the absence of the pressure of coercive participation, respected for our differences and embraced for our shared experiences. Here we must not forget that all antidotes contain a little poison: the platform also shapes our behavior and there are those who seem "friendlier" or "more correct" than they are in real life. Nevertheless, I find myself advocating for these spaces; I contradict myself, entangled again in the fisherwoman's net.

If women bear a hypervisible scarlet letter in public—too much leg or not enough skin, too much lipstick or not enough makeup, always too fat or too dark, our hair too short or long or curly, either too femme or too butch, always at fault, always out of place, always strange and foreign to the (heteropatriarchal) norm, our very being judged and objectified and disciplined through our bodies—then perhaps there are moments when the absence of that flesh-and-blood body, when the body is masked by an avatar, can even be liberatory, anarchic, disobedient, and creative. And these avatars aren't created in a vacuum, but instead reflect an embodied practice. Go ahead, ask any woman from a threatened or colonized community how she became an expert in the creation of avatars in order to survive. I have seen firsthand how, in these spaces, participants feel comfortable asking or sharing things they wouldn't even dare at group therapy: by writing, they share wounds so deep and so hidden that sharing them in any other context would make them feel ashamed. In these spaces, solidarity is woven naturally—sometimes one-on-one, sometimes as a group—while resources are collected (not always but sometimes materially), knowledge and know-how are shared, and the most radical insubordination is uttered without fear of criticism or punishment. I believe that tools are transformed when they are collectivized and politicized. I believe, then, that there are ways of opening up fissures in what they represent: the necropolitics of a phallocapitalism driven to make us disappear in so many ways. And yet we stubbornly reappear, viral and plural.

If Twitter has become a space for denouncing sexist violence, it has also become a space where women and queer/trans people are verbally attacked in the most atrocious and troubling ways, and so these groups open up on other social networks for safer verbalization. If (clandestine) groups were formed in the seventies to discuss and exercise reproductive sovereignty, we now take advantage of these virtual, technologically-reproduced spaces to continue questioning the lack of

DISOBEDIENT TOOLS

safe spaces in real life, to continue organizing around our bodily autonomy and the right to choose beyond the enclosures of medical-capitalist institutions, to speak to questions of harassment, rape, and all kinds of domestic violence without fear of being retraumatized or threatened; but also to celebrate birthdays and milestones, share addresses and professional contacts, collectivize childrearing stories, spend moments of happiness and despair together, take part in personal and professional challenges as women or nonbinary people, distribute texts, publications, articles, tweets, and links to interesting websites, all through space-times that allow us to do so safely but also and always opening up spaces and times to meet in person. With the exception of some groups with people who live far from each other, which makes it much harder to find a location where everyone can meet, nearly all the groups I belong to also aim for physical encounters, precisely so they don't forever remain virtual.

Here we are, here we remain; *here* can mean many things, something different and specific in one moment or another. We hear each other's voices, and here *voice* does not refer to the sound of vibrating vocal cords, but, as Rebecca Solnit says, "the ability to speak up, to participate, to experience oneself and be experienced as a free person with rights." A safe space, but not in terms of convenience or comfort, as these are generally constructed at the expense of others: comfort and convenience are words that are overtly connected to the oppression of some for the benefit of others (the bourgeoisie, men who find all this so bothersome, and so on). A space that must question precisely those concepts we take for granted, always seeking to open ourselves up to that feeling of the possibility of speech, the most transversal enunciation imaginable, always questioning the way in which not only our bodies but other ways of voicing are disciplined. We must open up our imaginations to new possibilities in new media that are perhaps safer and radically more disobedient (or truly disobedient) than these Silicon Valley social networks and chatrooms (where, as we all know, Big Brother is watching). Here there comes to mind, as a truly subversive example, the Talea Community Network (Red Comunitaria de Talea), a cell phone network established in the Oaxacan town of Villa de Talea de Castro—seventy miles from the state capital—as a response to a lack of coverage and as radical resistance to the abusive, unpayable rates of Movistar and Telcel (the quasi-monopoly of one of the richest and most powerful men in the world, hacked/checked by an ultramarginalized community). Another important example can be found in the healthcare initiative of the GynePunk "cyborg witches" who, among other forms of biohacking, develop medical instruments out of technological "waste" for the self-administration of pap smears, engaging strategies from marginalized communities in India to disappropriate hegemonic tools as an autonomous method of self-understanding. These are ways of détourning technology that look to other horizons than those of white feminists in Europe and the United States. They are examples, in other words, of how we conceptualize, develop, and collectivize knowledge and technologies (here I use the word *technology* in its broadest sense) that, as argued by both transfeminists and the economist Angela Corsani, allow for an appreciation of the transversal nature of oppression, solidarity with the emancipatory self-organization of others, and a will to "commit to the rhizomatic connections between resistances and insubordinations." I feel that seeking out alternative ways of forming communities and communicating, of writing and telling stories, of weaving and unweaving tangled herstories (here I disappropriate this term too) is a good start, and a feasible one. I have already named a few examples that are tremendously inspiring to me. Here I invite you to contribute your own experiments and investigations, to instigate explorations and dialogues that speak to this issue in your own networks. So, when we see a woman (who defines herself as such) writing, what do we see? What will she write? What possible futures, what new existences, what free and autonomous decisions does she recount, what resistances does she describe, reweave, inscribe, and experience through her body and beyond? For many of us, if these political and material systems seem difficult to navigate, it is because the masters have attempted to cloud this knowledge, but I must stress the transversal examples mentioned above, which break down divisions of class, race, gender, and ability to reveal that this apparent difficulty or inaccessibility is a fallacious construct. Let's disappropriate the master's tools, let's rethink our language, our self-defined communities, let our voices ring out until we have managed to transform not only our bodies, but the political systems in which they are immersed and disciplined. "We begin to speak the language of the birds or reappropriate words," as Silvia Rivera Cusicanqui says. So let our tongues be disobedient. Where to begin? It is true that these ways of communicating are provisional and disappropriated (but never inappropriate), and I hope they will be the stones over which we cross the stream toward a potentially lasting transformation and a world where we can achieve the emancipation of all. Let us sharpen our pencils, limber our fingers, hone our typing skills, our coding languages, our *de*tamed domestic implements; raise our voices as frenzied singers, howling street vendors, and strange birds; release our rebellious imaginations. Let's create a *eu*topia, that is, a good place: a better world, here and now.

Valeria Luiselli

BLACK WATER

(Fragment of twenty-four-hour sonic essay *Echoes from the Borderlands*. Can be read aloud around any table, in the company of women of different ages.)

NARRATRESS III:
¡Presidente! ¿Presente? ¡Padre! ¿Presente? Ausentes.

CHORUS:
the missing story
this is our voice, the voice that misses
these are our bodies
and this in our arms is a wet round rock

NARRATRESS III:
¡Señor Presidente! ¿Padre? Ausentes.

NARRATRESS I:
The first time I saw an open-pit copper mine—in Bisbee, Arizona—I had only just gotten a copper IUD inserted. It

made me nauseous, dizzy, sick: the coil, the pit, the sick. The
pit is red and steep, a basin-shaped excavation cut sharply, a
succession of steps, a quarry, like ancient farming terraces Arabs
carved on hillsides; only, instead of layers of barley, wheat, and
sorghum that vanish into natural erosion or undergrowth, the
terracing in the copper mine layers sand over sand over rock
over sand, in a downward circling spiral—then ends abruptly
in black water.

SEMICHORUS:
This is a story of copper,
a story of trade, accumulation
of capital, a story
of violence;
mercury retrograde, mining,
a story of dogs that bark and then fall silent,
of bowels,
your bank accounts,
señores.

NARRATRESS II:
In the late nineteenth century, Dr. Marion Sims,
considered the father
—though perhaps he was the grandfather—
of gynecology, invented the modern
version of the speculum,
the instrument inserted in a woman's vagina
for inspection,
examination via
metallic or plastic penetration.

The word speculum comes from the Latin verb *speculari*
used first in military jargon,
meaning to look as if from above, from a watchtower, to spy.
Sims is also known for having invented a method to cure
vesicovaginal fistulas,
a painful opening between the bladder and the vagina.
What is not so widely known is that,
to develop the cure,
he operated a little makeshift hospital
in Alabama,
where slave owners brought in enslaved women.
He experimented on the women,
ruthlessly,
without the use of anesthesia,
sometimes using spoons and knives,
without even a notion of consent.

NARRATRESS III:
Judges! Your Honor? Ausentes.

NARRATRESS I:
From high above, standing behind a mesh fence from where
the full extent of the quarry is visible, I looked down into the
open pit copper mine, observed that hole in its center, full of
black water, and tried hard to imagine, made an effort to understand. What drives men to dig, and dig further, in other mines,
elsewhere, too: stone quarrying, strip mining, underground
excavation? What is it that drives them to peal the surface
of the earth, rid it of its natural overburden—rocks, weeds,
roots—and penetrate it to make tunnels, carve their way in,

deeper and deeper, and find in there, in some dark, dry or moist entrails—find what? A gleam, a promise, matter with a specific mass, something to inject energy into, with rage or with pain or with sadness, drill into it, hammer it, blast it, have it, take it, something to have and eventually trade, something to defend and wage wars for, establish settlements around, found a company and then name a town that might maybe spread around it, pick a president, designate positions, accountants, secretaries and undersecretaries, build an industry; promise partners, shares; and heirs, fortunes; dig deeper and dig more, multiplying the slave hands of men who drink weak coffee before daybreak and then too much mean alcohol after the day's work.

SEMICHORUS:
the pinche jornada laboral larga,
chak jou travay fosè

NARRATRESS I:
The miserable indentured everydayness, for some, or the bonded foreverness, for many others—all for what? For a sliver of that coveted chimera? For copper, coal, chromite, granite, gypsum, uranium, marble, bitumen, the mining pit wide open like a mueca, a grimace, a big toothless mouth laughing at the night sky or maybe crying at it for help, while the men return home at the end of day, after having found some of it or not found any of it, bussed or pulled or by foot, to eat a bite and maybe fuck their wives in the dark, with rage or with pain or with sadness.

BLACK WATER 151

NARRATRESS IV:
The oldest metals known to humans
—human hands plus human imagination,
Machination—
are gold, silver, then copper.

NARRATRESS II:
In the genealogy of the IUD, the three metals made lineage:
gold, silver, copper, in that order.
Except the first IUD.
The first one was invented in 1909,
by a German doctor, Richard Richter.
It was made of silkworm gut,
and was largely unpopular.
Then came Ernst Gräfenberg,
also German,
who in 1929 invented an IUD made of silver.
Gräfenberg had done research about female ejaculation,
which later lead to the conceptualization and coining of
    the term "G-spot"
—an accomplishment more in lexicon than in men's
    practical knowledge.
But the point is, Gräfenberg's silver IUD was short-lived
because he was Jewish during
the Nazi regime,
so before he fled the country,
they had already banned his contraceptive method,
saying it was
a threat
to Aryan women
(they meant: threat to un-reproductive copulation,

to sex just for play and pleasure,
a promise of pleasure
for women in general,
therefore a threat
to Aryan men in particular
but also men in general).

NARRATRESS IV:
Mining is a mode of accumulation, for some; and of dispossession, for most.

NARRATRESS I:
From a vertical shaft dug up by a single person, in search for enough silver to secure a family's livelihood, to army scouts and government prospectors seeking mineralizations, companies laying land claims, men taking over territory and displacing an entire population. Because everything seems extractable and everyone seems removable.

There is something, perhaps, that has driven men, for millennia, and I'm not sure if it has also driven women or will ever drive them—it's difficult to know, because all the institutions we still live by were created by men: government, army, universities, mining companies, the church. But there is something that drives men to make meaning out of nothing, something out of copper or salt or oil or mercury, and there is a small beauty in that, despite it all, there is beauty in inventing the value of something like copper, and making meaning with it, turning chaos into cosmos, giving order to shapelessness. A small desperate beauty in men imagining institutions and in fact instituting them, giving them a name and a form, writing them down in a contract, fitting a tie around the neck, sip of coffee, leave for work, and then living as if those things had always existed and were the natural order of the world. But also, there is so much violence, in any form of making something out of nothing. And also, who gives a shit about all their beauty, when the pinche jornada laboral larga.

SEMICHORUS:
a story of copper,
a story of trade, accumulation
of capital, a story
of violence;
mercury retrograde, mining,
your bank accounts,
señores.

NARRATRESS IV:
Arizona produces 65 percent of the copper
extracted and manufactured in the United States.
There are vast porphyry copper deposits
in southern Arizona and New Mexico,
and northern Sonora and Chihuahua.
Some geologists think that those deposits formed
when what is now North America had detached
from Europe, was slowly drifting
northwest across the ocean,
and then glided across a hotter spot in the earth's mantle.
The heat transforming rocks, molding them.

How strange to imagine, to picture it,
and then to think that an event like that would result,
eventually, in little men with their little lives
and their enormous sense of ownership claiming
    those old rocks.

Tia Oros Peters writes about ongoing settler colonialism in extractivist industries and how it targets, especially, indigenous women and girls: "... we are more than the miner's canary ..."

TIA OROS PETERS:
"... we are more than the miner's canary who are released into mountains to measure the shift from fresh air to poisoned gas. We are those mountains that are being desecrated, ripped open, raped, and exploited. Indigenous bodies are the casualties of war taking place over these many centuries."

NARRATRESS IV:
And how do you engage with indigenous knowledge in a way that is not extractivist? I don't know, but maybe you start by listening.

NARRATRESS III:
What is it ... extractivist?

SEMICHORUS:
the pinche jornada laboral larga,
chak jou travay fosè

NARRATRESS I:

All of us who have had copper IUDs inserted in our uteri—
were we carrying a coil extracted from Arizona? Chile?
Australia? Who was displaced from the land where that shard
was extracted and later inserted in us?

SEMICHORUS:
the pinche jornada laboral larga
chak jou travay fosè

NARRATRESS I:

Some months after visiting the Bisbee copper mine, I abruptly
decided to take my own copper IUD out, and did, in a small
medical center, in the middle of a busy work trip—the gynecol-
ogist that craned her wrinkled neck forward, then between my
wide-open, reticent thighs, asked why. She was talking directly
to my cunt—why?—and behind her was an enlarged, generic
photograph of a white orchid.

The copper was making me deranged and sick, I could feel
it. I spoke to many other women who had also experienced
alarming reactions after having had an IUD inserted, only to
be told by their doctors that copper was safe, that there must be
something else wrong with them; nothing wrong with copper.
I was a mine pit, all dug up and steep and eroded in spirals, I
wanted to tell the doctor, as she inserted the cold beak of the
speculum in me, its little metal springs squeaking as the blades
opened up inside.

Why did I want to take it out? she insisted.

Because it makes me bleed too much, was the only explanation I gave. I spoke directly at the enormous orchid behind

her. An acceptable enough explanation, I suppose, to which she nodded, performing the extraction in one jerk, after which I paid and said thank you, Doctor.

NARRATRESS III:
Doctors! Chairmen of the Board! Ausentes.

NARRATRESS I:
Almost as soon as I had the copper removed, the little coiled fucker finally extricated, I began to even out, found temperance, perhaps, on some days, even some happiness. Like a mine at last left alone, abandoned, all the parts of me that had been feeling too sharply cut, angled in so many painful bends, began to undulate better, ductile again, my entire body finally agreeing to some kind of truce with existing, being matter among matter, a mass that not only occupies space but inhabits it: beds felt comfortable again, showers got longer, food more interesting, conversations more patient, and desire, once more, the wild undercurrent either loose but interiorly contained, or released sudden, abundant, unpredictable.

Perhaps because I was feeling better, when I returned home from that trip, felt sturdy again, well centered—thus ready, also, to stray toward pleasure—I smoked a joint with a lover, a good lover, and then had sex with that same lover, no condom, my open thighs not at all orchid-shaped this time. Predictably, I had to take the day-after pill and was sick and weak and felt deranged all over again.

BLACK WATER

NARRATRESS IV:
Geology is all about rocks and drift, therefore
extraction, therefore
chain-gangs, therefore
forced relocation, therefore
dispossession, therefore
displacement, therefore
drift and rocks.

NARRATRESS I:
Weeks passed and I realized my period was late, two days, four
days, six: I was worried, unsure if there was life growing inside
of me or maybe I just had a bad flu. I asked myself through all
those days, across all those days, while I waited for my body
to bleed, sitting on the toilet seat, each time I peed, checking
toilet paper for signs of red or brown or at least pinkish, but
nothing, no sign of it, asked myself if I would want to carry
another life into the world, ever again, into this world, with this
lover who was maybe not such a good lover, or with any other
lover, I had no more space in my life for more lives, but my
breasts were swelling, but my underwear remained insistently
unstained, but how could I not let it happen if it happened,
if life had happened, how would I dare end it—not morally
speaking. Or am I, unwillingly, morally speaking? Whose moral
structures speak in me, through me?

SEMICHORUS:
if I were to be pregnant again, what then,
but if I wasn't pregnant, also, what then
what then when then what

                                                    accumulation
                                                         violence
                                             mercury retrograde
                                                        señores.

NARRATRESS I:
I'd had an abortion once before, when I was very young and at
a time when it was illegal. I was first given two pills that made
me bleed brutally for days: during class, walking down the
street, while asleep. I had never seen so much blood. The pills
didn't fully work, and the man who performed the follow-up
ultrasound made me look at the image on the screen. He said:
Look what you have done, you tried to get rid of it but it's still
there, a cadaver, living inside you, well done. It was determined
that the next step would be to vacuum, and that is what they
did, without the use of anesthesia, in a metal bed, the speculum
deeply inserted, my mother by my side, holding my hand tight.

                                                          CHORUS:
                        this is a story of the missing, the missing story
                                    this is our voice, the voice that misses,
                                                    these are our bodies,
               and this in our arms is a vacuum cleaner full of pain.

NARRATRESS II:
Later, in 1934, a Japanese doctor,
Tenrei Ota,
developed an IUD made of gold.

It was called the Pressure Ring
—a name that has something of "engagement" and
 something of "corset."
It didn't last, so end of story.

NARRATRESS IV:
An element in the periodic table,
atomic number 29,
named Cu, for *cuprum*, in Latin, and perhaps,
earlier, from the Assyrian *kipar*—
but who knows.
In Roman alchemy and mythology,
copper was associated with the goddesses Aphrodite
 and Venus.
And I'd like to know why.
Copper, they say, runs through the very bowels of the earth.
Mineral veins, that run deep underground, hold copper.
And so, men mined copper.
But I'd still like to know why.
Copper, along with gold and meteoritic iron,
are the oldest metals known to man,
according to several encyclopedias.
And to women?
I don't know, they don't say.
They say there are Egyptian vessels made of copper
 from 4900 BC.
And copper beads eleven thousand years old were found
 in what is today Iraq.
And all of that was fine: rings, necklaces, bracelets, vessels.
But then men discovered that copper had conductive
 properties.

160   VALERIA LUISELLI

It conducted heat and electricity.
(And maybe that's why it's associated with Venus
   and Aphrodite.)
And because it had conductive properties it was used for
the telegraph, electric light, refrigerators, trains, microwaves,
airplanes, rockets, missiles, cluster bombs.

NARRATRESS I:
I wasn't pregnant. My period came, late but it came, with
the pain and with the almost full moon, laying its thick fog
over mood, dimming perspective, shortening the breadth of
patience and blurring the contours of ideas. The endometrium
was slowly expelled, first pink, then with brown debris-flakes,
sediment, sanguaza; then a wondrous purple, thick and almost
gelatinous; then the clots, expelled with spasmodic moans of
the uterine muscles, and hushed with ibuprofen; then a lighter
fluid, red and alive; and finally some stray droplets, diluted,
transparent, defeated. Of all the organs, the uterus is the most
Sisyphean, always cycling, tirelessly layering membrane over
membrane in its concave pit.

NARRATRESS III:
In class they said that the universe
was made of matter and energy.
Matter is anything that has mass and occupies space.
And energy is what causes a change of state in matter.
They said that.
There is potential energy and kinetic energy.
They said that, too.
Small things, like atoms or molecules are held together

BLACK WATER   161

by potential energy, energy that is stored inside things.
Kinetic energy is the energy of an object in motion.

NARRATRESS I:
I suppose that, after menstruation, after that copious release
of matter, the uterus begins to slowly shape itself back into
an empty, open space. I sense it, that vacuum, sometimes just
a hint of it: Kierkegaard, motherfucking poser; and as Carla
Lonzi says, "sputiamo su Hegel," let's spit on Hegel.

Other times I know it, entirely, with vertigo and with fear,
the pit I hold inside. I would like to look inside myself and feel
what some hypothetical man in the Arizonan 1800s might
have felt peering into the new open-pit of the Copper Queen
Mine: possibility, project, future. But instead, I see only doubt,
black water.

Maybe doubt is another kind of drive, a different form of
energy. Not one that carves terraces into hillsides or founds a
company and a town or signs trade agreements. Doubt does
nothing like that, but it is a drive, internal, molecular maybe,
a potential energy that grows in silence, swells, and becomes.
Doubt is like copper and endometrium: matter in the inevitable and circular process of becoming, giving. Doubt doesn't
make anything, but it is there to be made into something. Or
there to be left alone, palpitating.

SEMICHORUS:
mercury retrograde
bowels
your bank accounts,
señores.

NARRATRESS II:
In the 1960s, a gringo
doctor named Howard Tatum,
invented a device in the shape of a T,
T for Tatum maybe.
He thought a T would better adjust to the uterus.
He partnered with a Chilean doctor, Dr. Zipper,
who in turn discovered that copper was an effective spermicide,
and could be added to the plastic skeleton
    of the T-shaped device.
T-shaped models have a surface area of 380 mm^2 of copper.
150 million women in the world use a copper IUD.

NARRATRESS IV:
Side note: Chile is the world's leading producer of copper.
Other side note: the USA orchestrated its military coup against
Allende, after he nationalized copper mines.
Other-other side note: copper surfaces are said to repel virus,
and its price is trending upward.

NARRATRESS II:
It is possible, though this is not something confirmed
by any source, whatsoever,
that that same Dr. Zipper is related
to the inventor of the mechanism by which
little metal teeth
hook into little metal hollows,
aligned in a ladder pattern,
and pressed into each other by a slide that
glides up and down that ladder,

BLACK WATER

the whole thing a mere means to the end of opening
and closing
Zipping
unzipping
the boundary —cotton, denim, polyester—
that divides our naked bodies from the outside world;
flies, especially.

NARRATRESS I:
Men zip their flies, up and down, several times a day, up and
down. In public bathrooms, in motel rooms, in their solitary
apartments, unprompted or incited, alone or in company, the
zipper a door and a window. I remember the boys, when we
were teenagers, that forgot to zip up their fly after going to the
toilet and came back into the classroom, a sliver of their boxers
visible, and it was easy to imagine and hard to concentrate on
anything else, was it dark brown or pinkish, was it curved or
did it hang straight down, were there hairs around it yet, what
color, and would it grow in our palm if we enveloped it, but
how should we hold it, soft or tight? And then there were the
men, older men, riding the bus or the subway next to us, who
suddenly unzipped and sworded a sad, erect threat at us, and
if they were close enough they made sure it touched our knee
or shoulder. Later, the men in bars or parties whose breath we
wanted to feel close to our faces and whose zippers we played
with, fingertips only, or not even, just a rub, a friction of our
hips or knees against them. And those whose zippers we didn't
even notice we had already unzipped, because our hands were
deep into the elsewhere of pleasure, feeling creases, crotches,
traceable veins and tightened testicles, the head of it swollen,
ready. And then the men who caught us off guard, even if we

trusted them, sometimes especially if we trusted them, and unbuckled, unzipped, held our necks tight, too tight, pulled our hair and hated our faces and injected us with all their anger and pain, and filled us with fear, spit, and a self-disdain, lifelong for some of us, robbed of our right to pleasure, men whose zippers are the dead end of all the alleys we fear, and the beginning of all the corridors, bureaucratic or metaphysical, same thing, where we will either get lost, or not get lost, but which we will roam endlessly, in search of the body we were before that day, the day before that day.

SEMICHORUS:
we were before that day, the day before that day,
a mountain,
a story of dogs that bark and then fall silent.

NARRATRESS III:
Mamás, presentes.
Hermanas, presentes.
Abuelas, presentes.
Nosotras, presentes.

CHORUS:
This is our voice, the voice that misses;
these are our bodies,
and this in our hands is a wet round rock.

Ytzel Maya
tr. Julia Sanches

I AM HUNGER

hollow   you
the other calls
love assembles
two once once only

—Susana Thénon,
tr. Renata Treitel

PREFACE

Three floors. The first is reserved for the family business, for the metric tons of cement, for the rods, power, and water but not the affection, for the connections, building supplies: this is a house that makes other houses; the second floor, where darkness doesn't enter but hides in the large window facing the garden, a balcony, green against blank space, the first plants I seeded, which died to make way for other plants; the last is for the bedrooms, the refuge of slumber, the shouting that preceded us and that I don't remember anymore. It's nighttime. We moved in just a few days ago; my siblings have gone to bed, and my mom and I are in the kitchen hallway. This house was once a courtyard. My dad built the roof and the bedrooms. Years later, lightning would strike that very roof and shoot through his body, narrowly grazing his hair and skin, its force dampened by the tar coating the beams. Survival. We knocked down some of the walls and built others. Other streets in Ciudad Nezahualcóyotl were laid out in a straight line along the avenue, back when everything was mud and the sepia pictures were tied to pieces of memory, vestiges of punk and rock, patent leather, studs, white socks, and black shoes, I'm told, high boots, Víctimas del Doctor Cerebro, Los Mierdas, pirated Sex Pistol shirts, mementos that are now the beginnings of a bedroom community. Home. This kitchen is actually connected to the living room and dining room. It feels like it's in the way. To me, the periphery is the center. I've never set foot on the metro or walked on major avenues, but I have been to the ocean. My mom takes out a pair of scissors to snip a piece of red fabric tied tightly around my wrist. It's been cutting off my circulation for days. In my memories of this, she mumbles something about being born a woman, about keeping your legs closed and palms above the table, don't touch yourself there, be careful with people, with silence, with men, particularly with men and silence, scream, I'll teach you how to scream, I'll teach you all about life and being a woman, she says while trying to slip the blade between my skin and the poorly woven fabric.

Snip.

Blood.

The fabric and the flesh.

We learn to ask ourselves for forgiveness; I, too, make mistakes, I'm not perfect, I'm a mother, I'm a daughter, and I cut you and bleed you and ask for your forgiveness.

We accept responsibility after the consequences.

But never mention it again.

"This is something that is incurable and will never be cured no matter how many years go by. True, we have a lamp on the table again, and a little vase of flowers, and pictures of our loved ones, but we can no longer trust any of these things," wrote Natalia Ginzburg. I'd like to think—and tenderly, I convince myself—that this piece of writing, this text about my body, isn't a home but a potential future. That there are still flowers here, as well as the faces of my loved ones.

My wrist is still scarred.

I

My first memory may be a dream in which my parents teach me to walk from one end of the living room to the other, my first steps. In the memory, I can barely tell the floor from my body, though from a distance—the hindsight of memory—I try to differentiate them while moving from one armchair to another. My memories are full of flashes that don't let me distinguish the objects around me from who I was in that moment. Those steps were the first time my body managed to settle into itself and tackle the world around it. My mother's outstretched arm was mirrored in my father's, which waited for me to return, as if we were all united in the cause of my legs being in motion: this is my body, I tell myself, a body I don't remember having. Maybe this is why the remembrance and its movement feel more like a dream than something that really happened. Both body and dreams are hard to delineate—unlike weight, the sex a child is assigned at birth, the lines of our skin when we draw ourselves. All we are left with is the constant of having been there, of having slept, of being present in a specific place, in a time and a space: being the resident ego while simultaneously being the dream ego. Being a body.

This memory is pure light.

Being a sick body.

I think of all the possibilities of language and how they are enmeshed with corporality—this is how we create the world. When we write for the first time, *mi mamá me mima*, we don't think of all the possibilities contained in such a simple clause: the alliteration, the way the lips press together to say it, opening and closing; the way the letters curve, hand against paper, fingers around a pencil; the error. Joining the words together as we would in speech, writing *mimamámemima*. Because where should they—the spaces, the breaths—go? Who decides what constitutes an error? A maternal reading, writing from the body, a text: a turn of phrase that conceives.

I'm writing a research paper on the affective turn and the perception of lesbian desire around issues like the body, gender, and violence. I write: femicide, lesbofemicide, acuerpar,[1] phallogocentrism, invisibilize, lesbophobia. Every single page of my Word document becomes a succession of red squiggles, of terms the system recognizes as errors. The science of language gives sense and meaning to these words in an emancipatory gesture whose morphology describes us while at the same time naming the world. Though it hasn't caught up with us yet. It wasn't enough for us to fill pages with our woman-names, the proper names we inherited from our grandmothers, or the names we hid and substituted for others; sprouting beans and helping them grow wasn't enough, nor were the eggs painted to look like babies, or the many times we read aloud select poems by Rosario Castellanos we had to learn for graduation and then promptly forgot. Language has forgotten us. We are

---

1. Translator's note: The word *acuerpar* has a broad meaning in activist circles and feminist movements. In an essay on the website *Suds (Internacionalisme Solidaritat Feminismes)*, feminist Lorena Cabnal defines *acuerpamiento* or *acuerpar* as "the personal and collective action of our outraged bodies in relation to the injustices suffered by other bodies [that] come together to provide each other with political energy to resist and act against multiple patriarchal, colonial, racist, and capitalist oppressions. *Acuerpamiento* generates affective and spiritual energies and breaks down barriers and enforced time. It provides closeness and collective outrage while also revitalizing us and giving us renewed strength, so that *we can recover our joy without losing our outrage.*" The Royal Academy of the Spanish Language only defines *acuerpar* (*a + cuerpo*, or body) with a single word: *apoyar*, to support. There is no equivalent English term, although the phrases "to put your body on the line" or "to show up" capture the bodily solidarity contained in the term *acuerpar*.

agrammatical women: we appropriate linguistic dissidence. Ours are the words *fault, error, mistake,* and *confusion.* How can we use meaning and its many cartographies—those coordinates lost to history—to carve out a space for ourselves in the places we left behind and the ones where we now belong thanks to the small things: systemic implosion, revolution?

ALL OVER THE city, pink crosses slowly clutter the medians. Every night at 8:00 p.m., cars and their horns drive around in search of missing women, desaparecidas. The State of Mexico was the first in the country to declare a state of emergency due to gender-based violence. Three years later, in 2018, the National Commission to Prevent and Eradicate Violence against Women made the decision to declare a second state of emergency in view of the high rates of femicide recorded in the region. My family has always lived here, between the municipalities of Ozumba and Tepetlixpa—where there is a street named after my great-grandfather—and my very own Neza York. Sor Juana Inés de la Cruz was born near that street. Amid the dirt roads, unfinished buildings, and concrete is a blue aluminum sign that reads *Calle Juan Maya.* There is a photo of me and my siblings under that sign. Three kids pointing up at the name of our great-grandfather, a member of the Institutional Revolutionary Party and former mayor of Ozumba, a man we never met and would never have voted for, a man I would almost certainly have marched against. I like to think Sor Juana would have done the same.

I've learned to inhabit and uninhabit myself based on the words other people teach me. I like to think about the potential of words to reflect our selves in other women, maybe even transport us to less painful places. "We tell ourselves stories in order to live," wrote Joan Didion. That sentence is tattooed on my right arm alongside flowers and sapphic snakes. I also believe in stories and in the language of being fed up. For example, my mom taught me that *girl* meant keeping my legs closed when I wore a skirt and that *girl* also meant I had to be careful around the teacher who drove my friends home after class at our public elementary school. My high-school principal taught me that the word *puta* meant I couldn't hike my skirt up to make it look shorter and that *hysterical* meant not letting anyone see the scars I'd once again cut into my arms. My aunts taught me that the word *gay* meant I was going to hell and wouldn't be saved at the Second Coming of Christ. I don't know when I heard the word *lesbian* for the first time, but I see it now while flipping through photos for that research project. They look happy; they're walking, maybe even running. You can't quite see the movement of their feet in this photo that is as still as their smiles, which are side by side, guided by the rhythm of their march. "Visible lesbians, free lesbians," are the words on the sign they're holding. It's 1979, and it had just snowed on the outskirts of Mexico City. I may never meet the women in this photograph tinted pinkish-purple by my monitor and the hard passage of time, but I peer at them in order to ask myself: What is this limit and what are these bodies, these words that strive to define them? Did they ever imagine I would see them from here and now while defending the words embedded on my skin? There must be a section in the dictionary dedicated to these kinds of queries. A field in lexicography open to the questions and also-unsteady certainties of the body: lesbian, visible, and free.

MEMORY IS NOT an absolute truth.

II

I read aloud, sixteen (or *seize*): "The body's a prison, or a god. There's no in-between." And twenty-five (or *vingt-cinq*): "If man is made in the image of God, then God has a body. He may even be a body, or the eminent body of them all. The body of the thought of bodies." These two texts are from *58 Indices on the Body* by Jean-Luc Nancy, a French philosopher who created an ontology based on the "we," which is closer to the end of ideology than it is to creating a new ideology or attempting to explain another one.

My friend Brenda reminds me of a poem by Héctor Viel Temperley:

I move toward the thing I've known least of all in my life, I move toward my body.

Marx, Engels, Simmel, Durkheim, and a short list of other male names who founded sociology as a science can see themselves in their theories through the word "man" and, depending on the focus and dialectic, through empiricism and rationalism: the idea of substance or matter; of the tangible or of a superior being, interstices of collective action. At the apex of sociopolitical knowledge, there are no feminine pronouns. There was no room for us in the science devoted to studying society. We women were a social body apart. A n – i r r e l e v a n t – n o t h i n g. Separate.

III

Hunger is a typology of desire. Before I felt hunger, I had a body. I'm trying to find my way back to it now, to locate it again somewhere outside what I conceive as matter. My flesh is not my flesh but the flesh of those who observe me; my bones are no longer bones if not one with my flesh. I have trouble breathing when it's cold and am terrified of the purple shade of my hands. The thing that most encumbers me is the lesbian closet and living with the desire for hunger, an empty stomach, a sense of lightness, and yet with the extra weight of those forgotten boxes, of having been born a woman in Mexico. In her pandemic diary, Cristina Rivera Garza took a cue from Sara Ahmed when she wrote that "in a disembodied environment, the natural place of furniture is that of discretion if not the most cunning invisibility." One aspect of the insurrection that implies opening closet doors is stepping outside the circle of discretion. Making the body a cumbersome piece of furniture.

I started reading about the body and about dissident desire as part of another understanding of the body that was nearly identical to my own in Amélie Nothomb's *The Life of Hunger*. This is the site of one of my greatest fears, triggered by the beauty mandate. I learned how to throw up quietly at the age of fourteen. I discovered countless ways to eradicate hunger. I learned about calories and started counting them. Three hundred, not one more. I underlined this sentence in Nothomb's book: "By hunger, I mean that terrible lack within the whole being, the gnawing void, the aspiration not so much to a utopian plentitude as to simple reality: where there is nothing, I beg for there to be something." The things we underline in books reflect us from forgotten angles. We return to them as the women we no longer are and sit beside ourselves to read the women we once were.

When living with voluntary hunger, the words *desire, food,* and *satiety* cease to exist: the genetic of meaning shifts to a different, more painful plane. Through hunger, the text, and the body, Nothomb and I were one. I—as when she narrates herself through the body of a man gazing at a woman who is sublime—was God. Nothomb contains a kind of desire that never comes to be. An incomplete desire. Jean-Luc Nancy would agree with me. Philosophy and academic thought on the body and ethos—the process of inhabiting ourselves through customs and reasons for being—come from the need to articulate identity by questioning our situated existence and our relation to the broader social context. The body seems to me, and this is a shame sometimes, an unavoidable entity. Through our bodies, we signify the world. Donna Haraway writes that the body, or rather the study of political thought around the body, is a vector of tensions between social order and everyday life, technology and symbolic order, political representation and personal space, and science and ethics. Through text, our bodies respond to different ways of finding ourselves in the narrative spaces of history, shaking off the natural idea of being woman. How do we rise up against concept and class, slavery and ownership? In principle, there is no space in this revolution for the domestic angel, the feminine mystique, or the myth of womanhood. The body transforms socially, leaving a trail of questions; these are the basis for establishing and discerning different types of bodily meaning that are not only political and territorial but also encompass cultural practices and world languages. From this inhabited space, we can begin to reject the patriarchy's social, ideological, and economic power. Haraway says as much in *A Cyborg Manifesto*:

> The home, workplace, market, public arena, the body itself—all can be dispersed and interfaced in nearly infinite, polymorphous ways . . . The boundary is permeable between tool and myth, instrument and concept, historical systems of social relations and

historical anatomies of possible bodies, including objects of knowledge. Indeed, myth and tool mutually constitute each other.

Existing and having a body is an evocation of our own memories and the memories of others, vestiges of the fact that there was once something somewhere: being in the world in order to inhabit oneself with all the traits and definitions one is given.

The body was placed at the center of social studies and the humanities a mere twenty or thirty years ago. My concept of the body came and settled into the representation of a conceptual space that transcends, moving toward the redefinition of the natural/social paradigm, as well as the binaries material/discourse and object/subject. Inhabiting the self as a way of being and existing can also be framed as being inhabitable in the text. We can be one in our own bodies. We can inhabit ourselves through these modes and conditions of existence, which change and are resignifiable to ourselves. This is why I keep writing.

I delve into memory using this text and the texts of other women, the grouping that we are. The archive should be our best weapon against forgetting, against this dread—the fear of disappearing from official memory; our bodies as texts, as articulatory material against fracture and in favor of the impossibility of collective amnesia. Stories about the political body are an exercise in representation: they are told because it exists, and because this is what topples hegemonic views about the body. Narrating through the political, and through its diversities and divergences, can't and should not uphold a one-dimensional gaze on the body. A new open dialogue: a body-text, which implies a body-draft that was once a blank page; that is, new possibilities of writing, of inhabiting ourselves.

I WONDER IF Amélie Nothomb also tied a red ribbon around her wrist after promising herself she would never weigh more than a hundred pounds.

IV

The companion lovers are those who, violently desiring one another, live/love in peoples, following the verses of Sappho, "in beauty I will sing my companions." The companion lovers gather from lesbians all of the culture, the past, the inventions, the songs and the ways of life.

—Monique Wittig and Sande Zeig,
Lesbian Peoples:
Material for a Dictionary

We lie perfectly still in bed as we wait for one to land on us. We're naked and haven't showered in two days. Our flesh is a living trap for sweat, summer heat, and the night that will later bring with it fever and fitful slumber with voices that emerge from the pillows. The woman next to me talks in her sleep. Her words don't make any sense; they weave into ideas I can't decipher and then settle into memory like some kind of numen that gradually vanishes on the tip of her tongue and lips. I like to call them sleep-words. That part of language only lovers understand, a kind of family lexicon not unlike Natalia Ginzburg's, but with the power of desire. Tender mumbling. "We needed to articulate a language that would displace the emptiness and silence we experienced in exile," wrote Virginia Cano in *Ética tortillera*. This exile is a way for us to tell our own stories from within heterosexual canons, grammars, and taxonomies, so that, from the other side, we can determine the coordinates of our counter-hegemonic affective practices. We're still lying awake. This is how we hunt the mosquitoes that flew through the window we left open this evening. She came up with this strategy because she is obsessed with killing them. And her obsession fascinates me. We wait and count to ten. We do it in French because she's been teaching me to speak the language. I'm clumsy with my r's. Un, deux, trois ... Our bodies wrote this story.

V

The reverse of the totality, the other, the nonsubject, a dark continent: this is how our bodies have been defined in the political narratives constructed by patriarchy. When bodies are said to occupy a particular location—the same nonplace occupied by most politically narrated female bodies—they are accorded an iota of self-consciousness, not only in relation to the text but also in relation to an identity determined by a society in the marginalia of male power and the canonic hegemony of literature. What is subversion if not the dizzying act of shifting this to the marginalia, to what had never been named, or to what had only existed through the male gaze? Positioning oneself in the center of the metropolis—in the textual center in relation to a phallogocentric society, that is, the sliver of evidence between the erection of the logos (king, law, voice; absolute ego, total ego) and the phallus (read: male privilege) as posited by Derrida—occludes and ignores the cultural hybridizations that arise from these creases and folds. I prefer to think about writing and the body from the margins.

We're trapped in an endless masculine language, in a thicket of cultural constructions that don't represent us. Until last century, women were exiled from themselves, incorporated

I AM HUNGER

into and circumscribed by an economy, a culture, a politics, and a desire that catered to male interests. Hence the importance of not only building political narratives through writing but also of carving out a political space for us. And we *are* building it. I believe that being a woman, a lesbian, while writing about the body, about the epistemologies that model different modes of writing and the hidden languages of dykeism, is a way of establishing a community through the text, which is no longer canonical but horizontal, confrontational, at once searing and painful, and yet also present in our need to name ourselves and write ourselves as other. I return again and again to the words that Gabriela Mistral wrote to Doris Dana: "The lives that come together here, come together for a reason. Then there are those encounters that happen but fail, those that get married, and they think they love each other, but it's a failure . . . We must nurture this, Doris, love is a delicate thing." I'm a lesbian in an academic setting conducting research on the body through a feminist lens and my own lived experience; I theorize illness and have the space and need for that affectionate hunger. I'll say it again: We must nurture this, it's a delicate thing.

VI

We've been in self-quarantine for nearly five months. She's in Culiacán. Over six hundred miles away. The first time we met was at my twenty-sixth birthday party, though I can't remember her face. We've toured the lexicon of Northern Mexico and Mexico City. I've learned how to say chilo, jalados, and fierro. We've made up an antigeographical demonym braiding Mexico City and Culiacán: culichilanga. She doesn't know this yet, but we're inventing a new language. *I mentioned you in my essay*, I write to her. I try to remember all the movies and TV shows we've watched together long-distance. We figured out how to sync our screens: we count down online.

three) show. one season. the intro song is by ana tijoux. we finished it in two days. a femicide. or various attempted ones. we get excited when they kiss. my belly ached at the end. i don't know about you.

two) movie. 85 minutes. céline sciamma. water and what happens under it. the shots and the women, always the women, in the foreground. it reminds us of the before times.

one) show. three seasons. we haven't finished it yet. two women. a detective and a hitwoman. unfulfilled desire. they're obsessed with each other. i still don't know if they've kissed. i thought you'd fallen asleep, so i stopped replying. i'm awful, you said, but you're a gemini with scorpio rising.

VII

I do my best to finish this piece while there is a pandemic outside. Someone on Twitter messages me saying, "we survive everything we've been denied, or been forced to be (do)," and then goes on to describe her eating disorder as a cage. In Mexico, nine out of ten anorexia and bulimia patients are women. Our homes are now locked down, and our bodies have become not only dungeons but also waiting—a crueler restriction than the space itself. I wish I could believe Jazmina when she wrote in a letter to Eula Biss that we aren't islands but gardens in the jungle, but I have a hard time not seeing myself as actually distant from everything vegetation implies, superimposed on a screen of the imagination bestowed on us by birds and their prisons—so close to one, but so far from the other.

PROVOKING THE DESIRE for hunger and no longer menstruating meant I was strong enough to harm myself on the inside and that the power of my uterus was mine. I've never felt as close to Anne Sexton as I do when I read "In Celebration of My Uterus." I take a chance at living and celebrating myself. *Welcome, roots.* I've sometimes thought that I write about my body because compared to others I feel like a sick body, at odds with everyone else's bodies, with only half the time, the strength, the journey, half of everything. But this is only half true: the body as a space is unstable, reflected on the inside and outside, like a very fine sap of what we claim is balance; an unalterable body that also hides, disappears and is disappeared, becomes paralyzed, is quartered, distressed, exalted, a habitable everything and nothing at the same time, where we remain and in which we belong to each other in a violent system, and from which we transport ourselves to a space that is affective, loving, and revolutionary. (Counter)history and history as narrated through feminism not only speculates and considers how we women will write ourselves, it also questions itself and forces itself to ask, always and from then on: What is the other woman like? How do I name her, and how does she name me? This impulse for self-knowledge comes from the need to make ourselves visible, to erase the borders of the patriarchal space: to locate ourselves and pinpoint the nonspace. To (re)write through our nonvisibility, through the thick and murky fog, in order to unmark all that is possible, to eliminate stereotypes, to identify ourselves again, to rewind the violent advances of phallogocentrism—which understands the world as homogenous and universal—and reappropriate a maternal knowledge born in ancient times. To step out of the textual limits and enact politics from these new spaces, to return and turn into our voice. I don't know if I want to be a good feminist or if I want to keep resisting from the comfortable praxis of my office. I don't know if one day I'll get sick of going out to march like it's a ritual or if the chants, the songs, and the choreographies will stop meaning something to me. But I am certain that the feeling of a hivemind is powerful: I found politics through writing and through the body I discovered my self in the strength of the word *vulva*.

VIII

THE LESBIAN BODY THE JUICE THE SPITTLE THE SALIVA THE SNOT THE SWEAT THE TEARS THE WAX THE URINE THE FAECES THE EXCREMENT THE BLOOD THE LYMPH THE JELLY THE WATER THE CHYLE THE CHYME THE HUMOURS THE SECRETIONS THE PUS THE DISCHARGES THE SUPURATIONS THE BILE THE JUICES THE ACIDS THE FLUIDS THE FLUXES THE FOAM THE SULPHUR THE UREA THE MILK THE ALBUMEN THE OXYGEN THE FLATULENCE LA TÊTE LES CHEVILLES LES AINES LA LANGUE L'OCCIPUT L'ÉCHINE LES FLANCS LE NOMBRIL LE PUBIS LE CORPS LESBIEN

Lesbians are not women, claims Monique Wittig. Deserters of our *woman* class, we are also survivors, not only because we violently inhabit a sexualized, feminized body but because we haul around a closet imposed by the myth of woman. I find it hard to believe there's an alternative to living this way. Wittig's ideas about heterosexual thinking and Adrienne Rich's

I AM HUNGER

thoughts on compulsory heterosexuality place us at the center of an assemblage of concepts that are even more beleaguered and complex. Being a lesbian means rejecting the symbolic order of things, but being a lesbian also means having an obligation to remain subjected to a way of life contained in the Law of the Father. Being a lesbian means being a body of doctrines whose basis is the difference between gender and sex. Being a lesbian means opposing the system that flaunts sociopolitical power. In short, being a lesbian is exhausting. Being a lesbian also means being hungry. I am hungry all the time—for desire, for the end of desire, for beginnings, for withdrawal, for solitude. I am hunger.

As a lesbian, I also encounter a part of my body that sheds light on other affective possibilities in order to create ties with other bodies and dismantle that silence. By recognizing and naming myself a lesbian, I am saved from that hunger because I am located in a body that's finally mine. Writing from the body and with this body is a kind of de-censoring. And within this approach to the joint, collective writing of dissident, lesbian affection I conjure Hélène Cixous, who calls heterosexual relations a "fool's game" and asks, "Who are the men who give women the body that women blindly yield to them? Why so few texts?" And the answer: "Because so few have as yet won back their body."

A return to our bodies is a return to originary ideas and their capacity for reproduction and primal transmission. They dwell in the texts we write, from the first word we say to our last reaction on Instagram. Fire, a smiley, and tears are also words. This return and understanding of the body, through a disparate recognition and another form of inhabiting it—one perhaps farther from preconceptions about the body and closer to what is meant by an emancipation from hegemony—is a kind of communication through text, a mode and technology of language. I hold fast to this radical tenderness. This text ceases to be a text in order to become a body.

Brenda Navarro
tr. Heather Cleary and Gabriela Jauregui

4 AND A HALF DIATRIBES
IN MEXICO CITY

DIATRIBE 1.

Don't call me *sister*,
  sister
  because you don't call a monkey, a rat, a fox
  sister
  you might
  adopt a puppy or kitten
  because they're willing to be domesticated.
  We're not sisters,
  sis,
  because you forget me when you shout March
  Like a Girl
  even as your shoe digs
  into my back
            when I can't see you.

  No needlepoint or picnic
  can give back

  What your father and your brother took from me.

DIATRIBE 2.

The heart, the lungs, and the esophagus are not friends.
    But they belong to the same body
        though they've never seen each other.

    The women who gather
    like cells do in lungs
              don't reproduce
              because they want to
    They *are*
        And they shack up
        all of them together
because they know (do they?) that faced with the *drug*
they need to be stronger more
      visible
      important
      defiant
      explosive
      triumphant
      to battle the weak bedraggled body
      they hate but want to conquer.

    The heart pumps
    pumps
    pumps
    pumps
    and communicates with the veins and
    peripheral arteries that

4 AND A HALF DIATRIBES IN MEXICO CITY

Build bridges,
not alliances
because they know
(yes, they know)
as if they knew
they are part of the immune system.

The esophagus chokes
on the cud ~~of lip service~~
Deglutition is a complex process
divided into three phases
acting in coordination to transport the cud

~~of lip service~~

The heart, the lungs, and the esophagus are not friends.
But they belong to the same body
though they've never seen each other.

DIATRIBE 3.

When you told me that your girlfriends held your home together
though you couldn't see it

the screen is small

the president applauded
the governor applauded
the police applauded
that guy on Twitter applauded
the soldier, your father, your boyfriend
applauded
and you got ten thousand Likes.

But your home
my home
and the homes of your girlfriends
are not the same home
My mother, her coworker, don't have girlfriends
only homes to clean.

When you and your girlfriends hold (each other) together
(over)
the bones of my mother

and other mothers

they shatter.

Their lungs
their arthritis
their exhaustion
know nothing of paid leave.

I don't know your girlfriends
Or what friendship means to you.

Because when you told me your girlfriends
took care of you
and you applauded yourself
like the president
and the policeman
and the reporter

I wasn't talking about our very individual homes,
or about girlfriends, or about Likes.

DIATRIBE 4.

Does it bother you, comrade
     That I want to know
               what it's like
   to be taxes
   currency
   gold
   a five hundred peso bill?

   To be the bad habit of being a man
   and to talk like a man
   and to shit like a man
   Three beers, two women,
   feigned monogamy.

       Does it bother you?

I want to know if you like being
     if you enjoy
     being
a soccer match
showing up all over the news
getting paid five
or twenty
or forty-five million
for scoring a goal.

4 AND A HALF DIATRIBES IN MEXICO CITY   193

Just for curiosity's sake
just to amuse myself
I want to
get to the bottom of
what drives you
what excites you
how does it feel
to be a coveted prize?

Is it a lot, comrade?

What a lovely poem, comrade.
                    You look uneasy.
What a stirring novel

My brother kissed me on the lips when I was five
No one'll give me a prize for that.

To be a gun
Do you like being a big, bad gun?
and shouting Go fuck yourself, comrade!
And him shooting back that his dick is bigger.

Are you devastated, comrade
That I want to experience it,
to live and know
what it's like
                To be taxes,
currency
to be celebrated by men
to piss like a man

to leave like a man
to be an absent father like a man
and to understand
        To understand like man does
                        To know firsthand

That you are a man more than you are my ally.

HALF A DIATRIBE.

The heart,
     the lungs,
     and the esophagus are **not** friends.

Neither are we, sister.

               And yet,

we hold the world together.

Jumko Ogata-Aguilar
tr. Julianna Neuhouser

THE STORIES WE ARE MADE OF

Like the dead-seeming, cold rocks,
I have memories within that
came out of the material that went to make me.
Time and place have had their say.
—Zora Neale Hurston, *Dust Tracks on a Road*

La vida no es la que uno vivió,
sino la que uno recuerda,
y cómo la recuerda para contarla.
—Gabriel García Márquez,
Vivir para contarla

OUR IDENTITIES ARE a collection of stories we tell and are told about who we are and where we come from. These stories affect us on different scales: our family, our town, our state, our country and continent. Many are beautiful, of loves won and legacies inherited. They speak of stars, landscapes, and how we came to be. They are the tales told on birthdays and anniversaries, those we hear over and over as if it were the first time. *Tell that one, mama, no one here knows it!* can be overheard at funerals to remind us of the good times we had with the deceased and at parties amid shouts and laughter, reminding us of what we share with those around us.

Others are harder, even painful to hear, recounting the violence and trauma done to us before we were even born. Some are so difficult to tell that they never are; one has to dig like an archaeologist to find them, to unearth just a trace of understanding.

They can speak to dispossession, forced migration, historical processes that affect us in unimaginable ways. There are also those family secrets buried so well they're only ever whispered in kitchens. *I didn't know, no one ever told me.* All these stories forge the image we have of ourselves, their presence or absence informing our consciousness and perception of the world. Nor can we deny the influence of what we see in public space—media representations and stereotypes, popular language, and the dominant narratives about communities meaningfully (though not necessarily consciously) influence the way we conceive of the people around us and even what is expected of us in public space. The possibilities delimited by these stories and representations leave a significant mark on us, as they show us what we are capable of (or not) and can even build (or destroy) our self-image. Do we believe them or not? What do we keep and what is better ignored?

The stories that informed my identity go back to my early childhood. Until the age of nine, I lived in a small city in California, where my mother and father were studying at the University of California on a scholarship. I knew that I wasn't "American"; we were Mexicans, and we had a different culture. We ate enfrijoladas and salsa and went back to Mexico during vacations to visit our family. We knew that we had to speak English at school and on the street, but when we came back home, everything reverted back to Spanish. I tried to make friends with the other Mexican kids at school, but I quickly realized that they didn't consider me to be one of them. They saw me as different, but I didn't exactly understand what that difference was. Nor did I have a common Mexican name. My classmates were named Samuel, Rosa, Delfina, and I was ... Jumko. It's not a name in Spanish. Then my parents taught me that this was because my great-grandfather was from Japan. A country that sounded strange and distant to me, but I incorporated it into my story without asking many questions. Japan, we're from Japan, that's it. And my mother has said that I knew perfectly well how I was read in public in the United States: *Mama, I'm Black.* I often heard the word *exotic* used to refer to me. My particular combination of ethnicity and nationality was perceived as strange, making me *exotic* to others, those who were normal.

The Royal Academy of the Spanish Language tells us that this word comes from the Greek: it defines *exotic* as "foreign or originating in a distant country or place and perceived as very different from one's own." It also refers to what is "strange, shocking, extravagant." In other words, it is the observer who determines what and who is *exotic*: what is *normal* in their space and what is not. This construction through the subjective gaze is intimately mediated by the hegemonic narratives of our society—the way we inevitably see through a lens of racism, classism, sexism, and ableism, rejecting sexual and gender dissidence. This is how the gaze of those around us assigns us identities based on the contrast between our corporeality and theirs. These differences are subjected to the most detailed scrutiny, and we are rapidly associated, positively or negatively, with common narratives and stereotypes in the collective imaginary.

The whitened Western gaze has historically defined what is *exotic*, transforming entire cultures into the object of its fantasies and misinterpretations. Edward Said, for example, defines the Western gaze on the cultures of the Middle and Far East through the term "orientalism," which he describes as "a way of coming to terms with the Orient that is based on the Orient's special place in European Western experience . . . [that] expresses and represents that part culturally and ideologically as a mode of discourse with supporting institutions, vocabulary, scholarship, imagery, doctrines, even colonial bureaucracies and colonial styles." Said also insists on the importance of this construction for the West, as it allows for a contrast with the East. It defines an "us" through difference from an "other."

I didn't know anyone like me during my Californian

childhood, anyone who looked like me, who also had a "weird" name. Yet I had classmates from all over the world, and I knew that several of them were also considered to be *exotic*. In a sense, that was where I belonged, in that shared difference.

For example, I was Muslim for a couple of hours one afternoon. I often played with my friend Mariam, and one time, while my parents were in class, I ended up going to the mosque with her and her family. "Don't say you're Christian because they'll make fun of you," she said with the utmost seriousness. I put a scarf over my hair like she taught me, but the bullying I feared never came. With my features, they never suspected I wasn't from some African or Arab country, just like they were. In the United States, I had the opportunity to get to know many cultures, languages, and cuisines, and this diversity made me feel that, even though I was *exotic*, most of the other people around me were too, so it wasn't a problem. Most of my classmates, friends, and neighbors also spoke a language other than English, just like I did. We all had our culture and we shared it with others, so being *exotic* wasn't such a big deal.

When we came back to Mexico, my parents enrolled me in a public elementary school in Xalapa, Veracruz. I didn't like having to wake up earlier and wear a uniform. The other kids made fun of me for my accent in Spanish; they called me an *alien* and told me to go back to the United States. I was still *exotic*, but now the word painfully set me apart from others. And that weird name, where's it from? You think you're better than us because you lived in the United States, don't you? The same ritual would be repeated each year when attendance was called on the first day of class: *Agata . . . Ogata . . . Jjjjumko? It's pronounced Yumko, yes, it's Japanese, I'm part Japanese.* After we returned from the United States, my paternal grandmother came to live with us to help take care of me while my parents

THE STORIES WE ARE MADE OF 203

were working. We spent the afternoons together and even slept in the same bed, so I heard firsthand all the stories from a side of my family I had not spent much time with until then. She told me all about her father, who was tricked into signing a contract at the age of eighteen that forced him to leave Japan and come work in Mexico. She would tell me a little more about him each afternoon, but also about her mother, her sisters and brothers, her life in different parts of the country, and how she fell in love with my father's father. She told me about her first pregnancy and how she was kicked out of her house because she was still single, as well as the last time she saw her father before he died. I listened carefully and asked questions whenever there was something I didn't understand or when I wanted to learn what eventually happened to the protagonists of her stories, as most of them took place forty or fifty years ago. These stories weren't just about our family; she also spoke to me of the most important events that happened in the town of Otatitlán, Veracruz—the Sanctuary of the Black Christ—and why they had been remembered: the arrival of the Black Christ, the celebrations in its honor over the course of the year, and the pilgrims who came from all over the south. She also told me about how it had been profaned by a group of men who cut off the Christ's head and how they all came to tragic ends in the years that followed.

My grandmother taught me our history as a family and as a community; she gave me the stories I needed in order to reaffirm that the town also belonged to me. I didn't feel like I completely belonged here, but I now knew where we came from and that I had connections, no matter how tenuous, to a particular place. On my mother's side, the stories that most sparked my curiosity were those about my great-grandparents. Pedro and Jacoba had eleven children, and even though I never met Pedro, I remember Jacoba as a woman of few words, one who rarely smiled. My great-grandfather had been the mayor of Tuxpan, Veracruz, and my mother spoke of him affectionately. What she most remembered about him was that, despite having dozens of grandchildren, he never forgot a single birthday, sending greetings by telegram to all those who had left Tuxpan. In the stories about my mother's family, women play an important role: my mother vividly remembered the visits of her aunts from Xalapa de Marqués who were elegantly dressed in the style of the Isthmus, adorned with gold coins and speaking Zapotec with my great-grandfather, though he never taught the language to my grandmother or any of her siblings. She also said that my great-great-grandmother spoke Nahuatl, but that my great-grandmother was ashamed of this and rarely mentioned it. We had Indigenous ancestors, but they never spoke of this on my mother's side. Their languages had been lost several generations back, and with them, countless family stories.

In my elementary school in Xalapa, they taught us stories of another kind. History. We learned about the great Indigenous civilizations (emphasizing their status as a glorious *past*, never speaking of contemporary Indigenous peoples) and about the "discovery" of America. About the great process of mestizaje, which had created the Mexican population as we know it today. They only ever spoke of mestizos, Europeans, and Indigenous people, and at some point during the tireless repetition of this narrative, I buried that understanding my mother insists had once been so clear to me: *Mama, I'm Black*. We're mestizos. We're all mestizos, we're all equal.

Middle and high school went by without any major questions about my identity, which was instead expressed through *teen angst*: black clothing and eyeliner, the latter generously

THE STORIES WE ARE MADE OF   205

applied. I was more concerned with my individuality than with my community, and my priority was to explore my personality rather than my racialization or my family history.

When I started college, I encountered a space that was entirely new to me: the National Autonomous University of Mexico (UNAM), in the capital. There were thousands and thousands of people my age coming and going at all hours of the day, and the privilege of studying at a school with such an impressive reputation across the country, even throughout Latin America, was overwhelming. Whenever I heard people in Veracruz talking about the UNAM, it was always with words and gestures of admiration—it was truly an honor to form part of this institution. In high school, I saw my friends meticulously prepare for the entrance exam for the first, second, or even third time. Anything to be able to study there. When my turn came, I was intimidated by the number of applicants I saw that day. We filled every classroom in the school at forty people per classroom in a four-story building.

Discouraged, I thought there were too many of us, there was no way I'd make it. When I found out that I had been accepted, I happily thought about all my future classmates from across Mexico, imagining that we would be the majority. After all, the admissions process had shown me just how many applicants there were. I excitedly purchased a letterman jacket with the UNAM coat of arms: *The spirit shall speak for my race*.[1] At the welcoming ceremony, I was thrilled by the sound of the university cheer, trying to emulate those phrases I didn't yet know by heart. I was overcome by school spirit, anxious to start classes.

1. Translator's note: The UNAM motto was written by José Vasconcelos, a former UNAM president and Secretary of Education, as well as a major ideologue of mestizaje.

My first week was not at all what I was expecting. There were only seven or eight of us who weren't from Mexico City, of whom four or five were only interested in the film program, which has an indirect admissions process. Most of the others were locals who had studied in the UNAM high school system, whose students are granted automatic admission to the university. I also discovered that, in the capital, the UNAM wasn't seen with the same respect as it was in those places they referred to here as "the provinces," a term that became pejorative in their mouths. My crush was even ashamed of my UNAM jacket when we went out together: "Are you really going to wear that?"

My conception of the school rapidly dissolved and was replaced by another. On the one hand, I met many brilliant professors who fundamentally shaped my critical thinking and who introduced me to texts I probably would never have read had I stayed in Veracruz. On the other, the first time me and many of my classmates were sexually harassed by someone in a position of academic power was during my first semester; as I write these words, he still teaches in the undergrad program.

I confronted the History they had taught me in Veracruz and found a narrative that had been hidden in my basic education: the African diaspora in Mexico. I read about Africans who had been kidnapped, enslaved, and sold in New Spain and about the Afro-Mexican settlements that have survived to this day, many of which are located precisely in Veracruz. This information combined with my experiences in Mexico City—certain comments including the word *exotic*, which I had heard so often during my childhood; whether I was Colombian or Cuban; *where* was I from, because I certainly wasn't from here; whether what they say about morenas is true, qué guapa. The body, face, and hair that had always been with me were now subjected to outside attention; they were odd, odd yet

THE STORIES WE ARE MADE OF 207

attractive. I realized that here, at a different moment and in a different way, I was *other*, and that this otherness was due to my racialization. It was no longer an acknowledgement of my own identity—*Mama, I'm Black*—but the scrutiny of an outside gaze—*You can't be from here, where are you really from?*

During my first vacations back in Veracruz, I decided to carefully observe my environment through this new gaze, specifically in terms of what the people around me looked like. And so I rediscovered the African presence in the state of my birth; there were Black people everywhere, on the street, in my family—I was Black. The stories I had learned during my basic education in Mexico made a part of my identity that was so clear to me in my early childhood disappear entirely from my imaginary, and not just as a possibility for me, but for any Mexican. So many experiences that had troubled me throughout my life that I hadn't known how to articulate suddenly had names and definitions. As a racialized girl and young woman, I had experienced racist actions and microaggressions all my life, surrounded by messages at school and in the media that had taught me that I was less: less intelligent, less beautiful, less valuable than the white girls around me.

As I began to read more on the origins of racism, its history, and the ways in which it has been manifested in the Americas since colonization, I also began to see its effects on the present. There's only ever trailers featuring white people before a movie—unless it's a commercial for some charity. The comments about how beautiful *really whiiiite-white* people are. The disgust at the very idea of turning prieta.[2] I could even see the same racist expressions within feminism—which was

2. Translator's note: Dark-skinned, a term that is frequently used as an anti-Black slur but one that has recently begun to be reclaimed by antiracist activists.

something I identified with and felt represented by—where the women who received the greatest recognition were all white. This feminism spoke of the kitchen as a prison and of long hair as a burden we could finally rid ourselves of. It aimed to leave behind all those activities imposed by our gender: sewing and embroidery were dull tasks we should no longer perform. Makeup and the particular attention we paid to our personal grooming were also up for debate. Why should we obsess over our beauty if what we wanted was precisely to stop being voiceless dolls?

I took all these precepts seriously in the years following my discovery of feminism around age seventeen or eighteen, though I never dared to fully live them out. I never knew why I didn't feel entirely comfortable with this way of conceptualizing my liberation as a young woman, but as I began to learn about other feminist perspectives, particularly those developed by women of color—that is, Asian, Indigenous, and Black women—I realized that the movement I had known up until then was hegemonic white feminism. The ideas that worked for white women didn't work for my reality; it was necessary to think about other ways of resisting patriarchy. For example: For many white women, their hair can be a sign of their beauty and femininity, which is why they decide to cut it short and rid themselves of that burden. Yet many Black women have grown up with a complicated relationship toward our hair, as the racist society in which we live teaches us that it's "bad" because it's "messy," "wild," or "unprofessional." One of the ways I have learned to resist sexist and racist violence was precisely by learning to take care of my hair and not demand that it behave like that of white girls. To stop wishing that it was straight and that I could brush it, instead learning to untangle it carefully, patiently.

THE STORIES WE ARE MADE OF

By accepting and appreciating my hair for its texture, I was able to build connections with other Black friends and companions through empathy and mutual care. Spending the afternoon in conversation as they braided my hair and taught me how to take care of my new hairdo was part of this path of reconciliation with a body and a beauty that European standards have taught us are undesirable. I came to understand that appreciating my own beauty, as someone whose physical features do not fit into these imposed standards, is also a form of resistance. Although they had taught me not to see myself as beautiful, I reaffirm that I am, refusing to measure myself and reduce myself to their parameters and their attempts to make me feel inferior. Over time, I have even concluded that I no longer feel comfortable identifying as a feminist precisely because of the history and origins of the movement, a perspective that does not fit into my way of understanding and engaging in antipatriarchal resistance. I do not mean to say that feminism is bad or that it's not an important movement, simply that it has become a word that no longer describes those parts of me I wish to name. Nowadays, I prefer to speak of antipatriarchal thought and struggle as it defines what I confront without positioning Western space and thought as starting points for that confrontation.

My racist bias even affected my reading habits, which I had never closely examined. I mostly read white authors from the United States or European countries. The Mexican literary canon, for example, is predominantly white: Octavio Paz, Carlos Fuentes, Elena Garro, Rosario Castellanos. When I first read them, I was surprised that I didn't identify with their stories, that it was like reading literature from a strange and distant country. Gabriel García Márquez's novels were much more familiar due to their context and ways of speaking, the

Caribbean cultural heritage that was evident in his voice. The great works of Mexican literature reflected the reality of a context and culture that in no way resembled my Veracruzan family and upbringing, and I was troubled by the thought that my family and I were not *Mexicans* under these parameters. We simply did not possess these characteristics. I found no mentions of Afro-Mexicans or Asian Mexicans in these narratives, nor of any other identity that distanced itself from the discourse of mestizaje. I even felt uncomfortable when thinking of certain phrases that had once filled me with pride: *The spirit shall speak for my race.* But which race?

My African ancestors had been kidnapped and enslaved—entire aspects of their identities were eliminated, including their names, places of origin, languages, and so many of their cultural practices. My Japanese ancestor was also a victim of a euphemistic slavery of empty promises. He had lost his family, and he took a large part of his story with him when he died, as he left very little information behind. How do we tell the stories of these ancestors if so much has been definitively forgotten?

In "The Site of Memory," Toni Morrison suggests that it's not a question of solely depending on recollection to tell the stories of people's inner lives, but of incorporating the act of imagination: we engage in a type of literary archaeology by using a little information and some guesswork to reconstruct a world suggested by these ruins.

I have enjoyed the act of writing since childhood, though I gave it little importance. I simply enjoyed seeing a page fill with ink, with words upon words. It later became an exercise in self-knowledge, in unraveling ideas and feelings in a space apart in order to carefully examine them. Eddies of stories formed in my mind as all my experiences up until then came together, combined, contradicted each other, and failed to find

THE STORIES WE ARE MADE OF 211

a way out. I began to write down all the stories I had heard in each space I inhabited, through each voice that patiently and affectionately told them to me. At first I only wrote for myself, to preserve my family's memory, but then I began to seek out other spaces to share my stories. I wanted to speak publicly of other stories that weren't fully recognized and heard. To validate their existence, if only by affirming and revealing other ways of *being Mexican*.

Identity is a long, complex story that they tell us, which we adopt, modify, and retell in a new form. I write about who I am because my story encompasses the lives of my ancestors and the places they came from, their strength and their struggles. I write because this is how I keep our memory alive and confront the historical efforts to erase our voices and our collective existence.

I keep writing for me and my family. I also write with a voice of resistance—in the face of silence, oblivion, and the racism that dictates which stories are worth being preserved and which ones aren't.

My writing is a statement:

We are here.

They tried to erase us, they tried to forget us, but we're still here, and now they're going to listen.

Daniela Rea
tr. Gabriela Ramirez-Chavez

WHILE THE GIRLS ARE ASLEEP

2014

MARCH 27
We are born and joy weighs 7.7 pounds and measures 18.5 inches. This day will last a lifetime.

APRIL 2
You were two days old when your grandmother and I bathed you and you fainted. We pinched your cheeks, shook your little body, but you didn't wake up. You didn't move. You were wilting in my hands. We dressed you quickly. I wrapped you in a blanket and ran down three flights of stairs to the street. We rushed to the hospital. Your father and grandmother ran behind us with the keys, your birth certificate, insurance papers, and my purse. The doctors took us to a small room where they pricked you four or five times, inserting an IV in each of your little hands, then your feet. The doctors said I was making you nervous and asked me to leave the room. I refused. I told them if there was anything in the world that could make you feel safe it was me, your mother. The doctors said you needed to stay two or three nights so they could run some tests on you. They spoke of sudden infant death syndrome, CT scans,

216 DANIELA REA

blood chemistries, and other things we didn't understand, but which surely made them feel important. Your father and I demanded to stay, but we eventually had to leave without you. We left heartbroken and comforted one another. You stayed there naked in an incubator, crying out of hunger, pain, fear, I don't know.

APRIL 15

I woke up in the middle of the night. Ricardo, sleeping on one side and you, child, on the other. I hadn't slept in days. It all happened so fast—your arrival, my postpartum hemorrhage, your hospital stay, the sleepless nights, my breasts aching every time I fed you. I grew restless: "What is the point of having a family?" I asked Ricardo. Or maybe it was just a thought. Ricardo was still asleep, and I didn't try to wake him up. I don't think I wanted an answer.

I was full of doubt as I lay between you in the dark, in silence, because I was tired, confused, regretful, worried. I don't know. There I was, between you two, but I felt alone. Alone not only with that question but also in the enormity of life, my life and yours. Our little eternity. Alone in that vastness of time. Alone knowing that I would never stop being your mother and that I didn't feel like enough. For you or for me.

"What makes a home? At what point do we become parents or children to parents? When does a home become a home?" Brenda Navarro asks in her novel *Empty Houses* (tr. Sophie Hughes), and it's as if she's answering me from a distance.

APRIL 22

Fold blankets, fold little sweaters, fold diapers. Pull out a breast, pull out the other. Burp you. And if there's time, wash my face, look in the mirror.

APRIL 27

It's been a month since you were born, and I don't love you yet. We are still getting to know each other. I've spent these days looking at your face, your full moon cheeks, your expressions, learning your language. I remember that Nade called me when you were born, anxious to know if it's true that kids make you feel the greatest, most unconditional love possible. I said no. Not yet. It's something else: tenderness, body.

APRIL 29

I wasn't born a mother, and I didn't become a mother when you were born. I'm becoming one, slowly, when I wake up so you can drain my breasts, my blood, my energy. When I cry because you cry. When I leave you crying alone in the bedroom, because I don't know how to comfort you. And dawns like this, when I've rocked you to sleep in my arms and I am still alive.

APRIL 30

Carmen, a friend with a two-year-old, throws me a lifesaver:

> I've come to realize that to love a child is to love yourself. It is proving to yourself that you can continue to have or search for love without unhealthy attachments, violence, dependency, or neurosis. A lasting gift. But it's so hard when we have so many deeply ingrained habits and needs . . .

And, I would add, when we feel pressured to return to the outside world. To go out there and say: This is who I am, I'm still here.

JUNE 19

You slept most of the night. My breasts leaked onto the sheets, the milk stain shaped like an old map.

JUNE 24

Today is St. John's Day. We're at the window, waiting for rain.

JUNE 27

You turned three months old today. You like to look at trees and when we look into your eyes. You like George Harrison, our strolls in Chapultepec, and swings. I like to hug your warm body, run my nose across your cheeks, and think you're enjoying this life.

JUNE 28

After taking three months to decide your name, we finally registered you today. We picked out so many names but went with Naira, the one your grandmother chose on the day you were hospitalized. While we were waiting to hear from the doctor, she got on her phone, searched for names that meant "warrior," and came across this word. We aren't sure of its origins—some say it's Quechua, others Aimara. That it also means woman who sees, woman with wide eyes, memory.

JUNE 29

I don't know you.
(I should start by clarifying
that you're still a secret)

WHILE THE GIRLS ARE ASLEEP

I know your hands, yes,
their tiny grasp
where dreams are born.
Not yours, I mean
all of ours.
Not the ones we have for you, I mean
the ones you make us remember.

(From Marijo to you)

AUGUST 5

My parents got divorced when I was ten. They had a king-sized bed. When my dad moved out, my younger sister and I took over his side of the bed. I have a vivid memory of my mother watching movies late at night (with subtitles and the volume turned all the way down, so as not to wake us) while she washed our uniforms; all four of us attended a school run by nuns. I watched quietly from under the covers. Sometimes, I curled up between her legs and ate vinegar-boiled peanuts, the ones she bought at a stand just off the Pan-American Highway between Guanajuato and Irapuato, which she passed every day on her way to work. She might've only done this a few times, but it's one of my most vivid memories: my mother watching movies late at night while she washed our uniforms.

On those nights, while my siblings slept, my mother and I shared a sort of complicity. Our little secret. Now, that image of complicity has become one of loneliness. It's painful to remember. Maybe becoming a mother has me looking back on those memories in a new way. From a different point of

We are the hungry mouths that Nellie Campobello writes about in *My Mother's Hands* (tr. Irene Matthews): "We only had Mama. *She* only had our hungry mouths, with no understanding, no heart."

view. If I could turn back time and lie under those covers while my mother watches television, I'd say, "You aren't alone. We, your children, are by your side, we are with you, we are in this together."

SEPTEMBER 8

We are on a trip. We went to Monterrey for the exhumation of a young woman's bones because her mother needed another DNA test to prove it was, in fact, her daughter. Now we're in Saltillo, at a migrant shelter where two little boys, Jonny and Jared, play with you. Jared takes care of you, sharing his peanuts, potato chips, and pre-licked candies; he shows you around, pushing your stroller through the bedrooms. Jared is only four years old and has received death threats. I'm not sure what happened, but I think his father murdered someone before he was murdered and now those men want to kill Jared. To erase his legacy on earth. Jared is as much of a kid as you are, and he's already learned the words *death threat*.

SEPTEMBER 12

I read: "As mothers and fathers, we are far too alone in the challenging task of caring for our children." —*¿Dónde está mi tribu?* by Carolina del Olmo.

NOVEMBER 27

We are by the ocean, celebrating eight months of life together. At a beach north of Veracruz with grey sand and murky water. We are here to film a documentary, and while Gabo films the

WHILE THE GIRLS ARE ASLEEP 221

sunrise, you crawl onto the beach, eat sand, and rip the wings off a dragonfly.

DECEMBER 3
You got a new tooth today.

2015

JANUARY 6
It's almost midnight, your dad's at work, and I'm trying to write. You come crawling into the living room, over to my desk, use my chair to pull yourself up, and cry for me to take you in my arms. I don't want to see you for a while. Or hear you. But you keep pulling on my leg and crying. I ignore you and keep trying to write—you win. I turn off my computer, pick you up, and once again it's just you and me.

JANUARY 13
I was exhausted. I took you in my arms and held you against my breast as if to suffocate you, and asked: "Are you hungry? Eat, eat, don't cry or I won't pay attention to you." I was tired and needed to focus for twenty minutes to finish writing a piece for a deadline.

What am I becoming?

JANUARY 15
It's almost midnight. It's been two hours since I tried putting you to sleep, and you won't stop crying. You don't want to eat,

holding you does nothing. I can't take it anymore. I leave you crying in the bedroom. I pick up the toys scattered everywhere and clean the kitchen to buy myself time, to keep myself busy. I don't want to go back to the bedroom. I turn on the light and get on my computer to distract myself. I read an article about a woman, an exemplary student who recently abandoned her three daughters, the youngest twenty-one days old. You haven't stopped crying. At the bottom of the page there is a link to other stories about women who were convicted in the last few years of murdering their children. I read them. They are obscene, but slowly they take on new meaning. I'm not sure if I empathize with them, but I don't think the news tells us the whole story. I can imagine thousands of delirious moments: women in their homes, their bedrooms, their bathrooms, all alone. Alone. A woman can lose her mind at any moment, go crazy, want to run away. Now I'm the one who can't stop crying.

JANUARY 17
A friend writes to me:

> I've had thoughts like that and felt so guilty afterwards. Sometimes when I'm giving him a bath, he's not doing anything, and I think: it would be so easy to drown him, and it immediately pains me, it pains me so much, because I know he trusts me and I couldn't live without him. Or it would be a living hell. Where do those thoughts come from? How do we return to love after we reach our limit as mothers?

How do we return to love?

JANUARY 19

Carlos González is a pediatrician who writes books about child-rearing. In his book *Bésame Mucho*, he tells the story of a woman whose three-year-old daughter cries and cries and cries. No matter what the mother does, the baby cries. "What the hell does she want now? She wants her mother, she wants you." But she doesn't want you, he goes on to say, for the material security you provide or the biological needs you fulfill. "A child's love is pure, absolute, selfless," he declares, then asks: "Why don't you, as a mother, enjoy receiving this marvelous gift of absolute love?"

I don't believe him. It's hard for me to believe.

JANUARY 20

You learned how to wave. You open and close your hand like a starfish. Today we fell asleep while I breastfed you.

JANUARY 24

A friend and I talked about parenting. To him, his daughter came into the world to be useful, and to his partner, she came to be happy. I have so many dreams for you, but I'll keep them to myself. I don't want them to weigh on you.

MARCH 10

You are eleven months old.
You can stand.
You can walk from one place to another if we hold you.
You say "dis" when you want to give me something.
You point when you want me to give you something.

MARCH 15

A kid was run over today right in front of our house. He was riding his bicycle, and a bus hit him. He is dying as I write this. From the window, I see a white sheet and under it one of his bicycle wheels. An ambulance, police cars, a candle. I think about your dad on his bicycle. About all the days we say goodbye when he goes off to work. Today someone said goodbye for the last time.

MARCH 20

After spending all day yesterday taking care of you, my only plan was to Skype with Michel, but you couldn't sleep. Because you were tired. Because of your fever. Because of your tooth. You wouldn't go to sleep, so I had to cancel. I was furious and you were crying. Today, you are only body, cries, tears, screams, moans.

I reread *forgive me* and maybe what I'm trying to say is, I would do it all over again. If you read this someday, I want you to know you have yourself. As many times as you need, Naira. My daughter, my body, my tears.

Forgive me, Naira.

MAY 27

We're at the park. While you sleep, I read about a woman whose son is missing. The last time she spoke with him, or rather, the last time she heard from him, was when his kidnappers called to negotiate a ransom. He said, "Mom, get me out of here, help me." She managed to say, "Everything will be okay, son." The kidnappers hung up before she could say I love you.

You're asleep and I reread her words: "Everything will be okay, son."

The day we left you in the hospital, in other people's hands, and closed the door to that room full of incubators, I thought about those women. The mothers of the disappeared. Of how impossible it is to take care. To take care of you, children.

END OF JUNE

You took your first steps today. I had to work, so you stayed home with Lupita. When I came home and opened the door, she said, "Show her, Naira," and you took eleven hesitant steps into my arms.

JULY 6

A Monday. We stayed home all day.

AUGUST 17

On days like this, I remember your grandmother Rosario. She worked in another city and came home every day after a forty-minute drive in her grey Tsuru, always playing her Rod Stewart and Creedence cassettes. She always came home exhausted—so exhausted that she'd collapse into bed and fall asleep while we drew on her. Sometimes, we played connect-the-dots with her moles and birthmarks. One day, we used a black permanent marker. The next day she had to teach in long sleeves and pants because she couldn't scrub off all the ink.

AUGUST 21

It's 11 p.m. and I have to turn in a draft of my book in a week. You wake up, leave the bedroom, and walk over to my desk. You're hungry. I give you something to eat, put you in your highchair, and you watch me write. You finish eating. You get bored. So I search for something online to entertain you. On one half of my screen, I write about a woman who was tortured and raped by soldiers, and on the other half you watch cartoons. Sometimes, more than my daughter, you are a companion.

SEPTEMBER 26

We're in Xalapa at a conference about journalism and violence. Someone in the audience looks after you while I participate, but you get away. You walk through the audience until you reach the stage, pull yourself up on my lap, lift my blouse, take out my breast, and feed yourself. I try to pay attention to the stories about bloated bodies on mortuary tables, but you keep talking to me, stick your finger in my nose and laugh at your mischief. How can I talk about death

when you

. . .

NOVEMBER 30

I read: "What women weren't expecting when they answered the call to motherhood was to face more requirements for being a 'good mother.' Now, she is advised to go back to the days of natural birth, extended breastfeeding, cloth diapers, and hauling her children to every appointment and meeting (medical, educational, social).

What about our ability to choose? To use the little freedom we have left to decide what we want? I meet all the expectations Meruane outlines, but I don't consider myself a "good mother" at all. Naira was delivered by a midwife at home, I breastfed her for two years

WHILE THE GIRLS ARE ASLEEP

And to spend more quality time with them, thus reducing her independence." —*Contra los hijos* by Lina Meruane

2016

FEBRUARY 26

Naira, so much has happened in these past few months. So many doubts. A few weeks ago, you started pulling your hair when you get frustrated or angry. What can we do? Are we doing something wrong? Is this just another phase? In these past few months, you've also learned to say more words: botili, dragafly, letescope.

MARCH 14

After almost two years of breastfeeding you, I'm going to stop. I want to sleep at night and wear high-neck dresses. I

(that include co-sleeping with Ricardo and me), used cloth diapers, and, yes, I take her everywhere, whenever possible. I take her with me because Ricardo gets off work at midnight, my family lives in another city, day care closes at 5, and we can't always afford a babysitter. Plus, the babysitter lives two hours away by public transportation so she can't wait for me to finish a project, dinner, or drinks or she'll get home after midnight to take care of her own daughters. But I also bring Naira along because I want her to learn to be a caring, sensitive girl, and I think my job as a reporter allows her to meet people whose circumstances are very different from her own. Every time we board a plane or bus, we get dirty looks from other passengers. Every time I go out, I see more pet-friendly cafés and restaurants than kid-friendly ones. And I don't want this adult world to relegate my daughter and me to the dark, solitary corner of the domestic sphere. Yes, I would love to go out again with arms free, without a diaper bag or little girl, without having to chase her around the restaurant when I want to talk to my friends. I would love not having to cancel outings and trips, more and more often. But I've come to understand that going out into the world with my daughter is a political act.

want, I *need* to know my body doesn't (only) belong to you. But at the same time, how to explain this faint nostalgia?

MARCH 16

Naira, you're going to have a little brother or sister.

JUNE 3

I had a very strange dream. I dreamed that I was in love with my brother, that our mother knew and was bent on keeping us apart. She widened the path between us, invented a language so that we couldn't understand each other ... One day my brother set sail in a boat, I couldn't go with him for some reason, so I professed my love to him. He walked me to the bow, where I would jump off and swim to the pier. As I was diving in, he dove after me, but the tide and waves carried us away from each other.

I wake up. I think I'm scared of losing my sense of self, my freedom, whatever that means.

JUNE 6

I had another strange dream. We were on the beach getting ready to sail across the Gulf of Mexico. We got on the boat and started sailing, but when we let go of the sails, the wind pushed us back to our starting point. We docked and waited two days before sailing again. There were giant waves, storms, and a lot of doubt. Suddenly, two giant, dense grey clouds passed over us. Soon the sun would come out and we'd be able to raise our anchors, or so we thought. It started to snow. Snow on the beach, on the waves, white snow that made the plankton shine even brighter.

I wake up and we don't set sail. Your dad tells me that if I want, I could go to the ocean to have my adventures, that he will stay and you two will dream up your own adventures at home.

WHILE THE GIRLS ARE ASLEEP

JUNE 15

I've been crying for days. I'm going to have another child, and I feel like it will erase who I am as a person. But someone nearby hears me and hugs me: you won't be erased; we didn't erase our parents. They flourished.

JUNE 23

I dreamed that I was shipwrecked. I was in the middle of the ocean, far from the nearest shore. I started to swim but soon realized I couldn't keep fighting my exhaustion and the waves. So I gave in and the waves began to lull me. The ocean grew calm, and I spotted another shore. I swam and swam until I reached it. I felt at ease. I climbed over a wall, walked along the coast, and felt at ease.

I wake up and remember that when you were born, I had to find a new point of equilibrium. Somewhere we would be safe, somewhere you would fit and there would be more balance. Now that your brother or sister will be born, we'll have to find a new place.

JUNE 25

I read: "A new counterattack has been launched against women to lure them back into the home. The excuse deployed has an old name: children!"—*Contra los hijos* by Lina Meruane

No, we won't go back to the home. We push to work and care for our children.

JULY 6

You like drawing by the window.

JULY 27

I'm at my mom's house, the house where I grew up. I'm here to interview her. I want to understand how I was raised, but first I need to understand how she was raised. Every day for a week, we wake up in the early hours of the morning to talk before Naira, Nicolás, and Lúa get up. We settle in the living room, in the garden, or on the rugs with some tea, a notebook, and tape recorder. We talk quietly so as not to wake anyone. On one of these mornings, I ask my mom to tell me about the memory I have of her washing our uniforms in the middle of the night.

> Me: I have so many memories of you staying up late to wash our clothes . . .

> Mom: I wasn't unhappy, I had you children. Besides, even if it was late and your dad was caught up in his own things, he would eventually come home . . . and then I wasn't alone, alone. You all filled my heart because you were beautiful, studious, nice—and everything else, staying up late, washing, didn't matter.

> When I was pregnant with you, I was getting my master's degree. My life was work, housework, your siblings Caro and Luis, and looking after your father. Our neighbor Professor Piña once asked me, "Why are you up in the middle of the night? I can't sleep." It was the only time I had to do homework on my typewriter, but it wasn't so bad. I didn't know there were other ways to be a mother and thought it was normal to lose sleep, get up early, give everything . . . It was the only way I knew, so I didn't reject it.

> I need you to know that I didn't suffer. I get the impression that you think I suffered, and it hurts you.

WHILE THE GIRLS ARE ASLEEP 231

I worked my ass off, but it wasn't a burden. I don't feel like I sacrificed myself.

Me: Did you ever notice me wake up and watch you?

Mom: Yes, but I don't want you to suffer when you think about those nights, I don't want those memories to hurt you. For me, going up to the terrace at dawn to wash clothes meant seeing the moon and stars. And seeing you all well-dressed the next day . . . I didn't have time to think about being tired and I was young and strong. . . . My affection, my strength, my creativity multiplied because I had all of you.

At the end of each recording, you can hear the children begin to interrupt the conversation, first approaching us to snuggle between us, then asking for breakfast, then wanting to play. Until it's impossible to continue and we turn off the recorder.

My mother. "She would fly above her sorrows like the swallows heading for the place of no return, and always pushed her problems far aside." —*My Mother's Hands* by Nellie Campobello

SOME DAY IN AUGUST

I hate my life. My body. My mornings. I can't stand fighting with Naira for an entire hour just to get her dressed: put on your sweater, don't take off your clothes, diaper, and pants, over and over again. Is this what it means to be a mother? Daily battles over insignificant things? Every single day? I'm sure I could put an end to these fights if I just put my foot down and forced her. I feel like my life has become exactly what I didn't want it to be: being upset about everything, all the time.

AUGUST 24

I know that I can love you, Naira. I also know that I can hurt you. Like I did today. I was walking you to school, and I squeezed and pulled your arm because you were crying. I also know that I can calm down, stop in the middle of the street and hug you. That I can talk to you in a different way and feel how we calm down together. I can be and do both things.

SEPTEMBER 13

You're going to be a girl.

A few years later, I read a passage in Brenda Navarro's *Empty Houses* that helps me put into words what I'm ashamed of:

"Shut up with your ore, ore! I said, dragging him by the hair under the cold shower where he began to scream . . . as if searching for someone. He was sobbing and started almost to choke on his own snot while the water continued to fall over him. As he thrashed about he pulled on my hair with his two desperate little hands and I felt like a total bitch. That's when it dawned on me . . . that somewhere deep down inside of him he was telling me I was a dick, an asshole, or something like that . . . and I felt so sad and I climbed into the shower to wash him as he deserved and I stroked his soft head of curls and held him. I didn't say anything but inside I wanted to apologize for all the shit I'd put him through."

SEPTEMBER 29

You peed on the floor after I told you to put on a diaper or go to the bathroom. You peed, so I picked you up and sat you on your potty. You were crying. Stay there until you learn. Cochina, dirty girl. You're a cochina. You don't learn. Cochina.

Why did I say that to you? Out of anger? Despair? Because I have power over you? To humiliate you? I'm so sorry, Naira. I'm so sorry. I feel so ashamed.

OCTOBER 1

We were on the rooftop playing with dirt. You got your face dirty, so I affectionately called you my cochinita. You stopped playing and looked at me with a straight face. "I'm not a cochina."

OCTOBER 20
Your dad and I wonder how you will make your entrance into this world, how our love will change. What will your face look like, what will it be like to have you with us? I'm excited to have you and Naira together, to walk down the street with you and proudly call you "my girls."

DECEMBER 1
Yes, motherhood is imposed. Our bodies are in the service of capital. Our bodies are exploited to produce the labor force. Patriarchy decides for us. Yes, all of that is true. But what about tenderness? And this inexplicable feeling I get when I smell you, when I look at you, when we cuddle? The urge to kiss you and look at you? The sense of belonging I feel when we hug each other to sleep? How do we explain all of this?

SOME DAY IN DECEMBER
Naira is with her grandmother, Ricardo is at work, and I'm home alone waiting for our second daughter to be born. I go through my diary, trying to remember what it was like to have a baby at home. I stop at the day I hurt Naira on our way to kindergarten. Now I remember that she didn't want to get dressed, she took her clothes off three times, we were running late, and I missed an appointment. I forced her to get dressed and carried her crying out of the house. I was furious, I wanted to hurt her. Maybe I thought about hitting her, wanted to hit

her, but I didn't dare. I squeezed her arm tightly. I also stop at the day I called her "cochina." I remember Naira looked up at me from the floor where she was struggling to put on her pants and said, "I'm not a cochina, mama, I'm not a cochina." She was only two-and-a-half years old when she had to defend herself from me.

I hurt her. I'm ashamed of what I did and feel ashamed to write this, but I want to record it. So I don't forget.

DECEMBER 19

Daughter, I've been absent from this pregnancy because there is a world outside. I've spent these months afraid that you'll erase me, that I won't be the woman I was before, that I'll lose the sense of balance I achieved with Naira over these past two years. But your dad and my friends have helped me understand it's not your fault. It's true, I won't be the same as I was before, but you're not the reason I'm scared. The root of my fears is this need I feel to legitimize myself, who I am, out in the world.

Silvia Federici puts it like this in *Caliban and the Witch*: "the feminist insight which refuses to identify the body with the sphere of the private and, in this vein, speaks of 'body politics.'" In other words, it's not me, it's the patriarchy.

DECEMBER 21

We don't get up. We stay in bed, watching how the light pours in through the window.

DECEMBER 26

Expecting . . . that uncertain verb.

DECEMBER 30

I read somewhere: "A mother's love is a one-way street."

2017

JANUARY 9

3:14 a.m. You came into this family, and we are more a family with you. In the middle of the night, untimely, and with a feline roar. Then you latched onto my breast and sucked like there was no tomorrow. Joy comes in a mold: 7.7 pounds, 18.5 inches.

JANUARY 10

Naira was there when you were born. She stroked my hair and brought me warm compresses to ease the pain. She held my hand to help me reach the end. I was on my knees, your father held me up and Naira stood waiting beside me. Two contractions, two pushes later, you were born and let out a cry. Naira smiled and laughed as she looked at you: "That's my little sister." She danced and sang, "Let it go, let it go," spinning around in our living room.

What is the point of having a family? I asked myself three years ago, when Naira was not yet Naira. Now, it's clearer to me. This is the point. To have each other, to create ourselves together.

JANUARY 11

Will this joy last, will it sustain us our entire life?

JANUARY 15

Starting all over again, so much crying, time standing still . . .

It's 4 a.m. and you've woken up several times to eat. I am not my own. My uterus, my breasts, my ears, are not mine. Only my eyes, which I can close to not see you. My uterus and breasts hurt. My ears can't ignore your cries. The cramps I feel when I breastfeed you remind me that this pain, my exhaustion, unites us.

> "As it grew dark, she would seat us all around her and give us what her hands had cooked for us. She did not speak to us; she was simply there, quiet as a wounded dove, pure and gentle. She seemed like our prisoner—I know now that she was our captive." —*My Mother's Hands* by Nellie Campobello

JANUARY 29

Days to remember. The smell of milk as I sleep between two pups.

FEBRUARY 5

Naira chose your name. We'll call you Emilia.

FEBRUARY 7

It's getting dark. I'm in the bedroom watching Naira and Emilia sleep. Ricardo is in the living room smoking a cigarette. We are together, but we are alone. All four of us, perhaps them less so than Ricardo and me.

> ". . . for I was lonely and wished to see people in whose faces I could recognize something of myself. Because who was I?" —*The Autobiography of My Mother* by Jamaica Kincaid

FEBRUARY 9

You are one month old today, Emilia, and I woke up feeling

like I don't know who I am anymore. Or I don't remember. Or I won't be myself again. I am no longer my own.

FEBRUARY 22

I asked Graciela, a mother looking for her disappeared daughter, if she has held any of the bones found in clandestine graves. She said yes. I asked her what it felt like. She said, "It feels like holding a newborn." You were in my arms, Emilia, when she told me, and I couldn't stop crying.

FEBRUARY 27

Yolanda the midwife came by yesterday. In a month and a half, you've grown two inches and gained three pounds. You devour me, daughter. You come from me. From my milk, my strength, my exhaustion.

MARCH 21

My body reminds me of my mother's body when my younger sister was born. Wide hips, full and warm breasts, hands covered in freckles. My body smells like her drawers did whenever I opened them to look for something—the smell of a body, a mother's body. I don't know what I was looking for in those underwear drawers, but once I found the letters we wrote to the Magi; another time I found a letter a lover wrote to her.

MARCH 29

I wanted to go to Raúl Zurita's reading. I arranged my schedule so I could take the afternoon and go with the girls. I got everything ready: a diaper bag, stroller, carrier, and our lunch. About half an hour before we had to leave, Naira peed herself. I changed her. There was still enough time for us to leave and walk thirty minutes to the venue. Just as we were leaving, Naira pooped herself.

I closed the door. I'd lost.

I put Emilia down on the sofa. I took Naira to the bathroom, took off her underwear, washed her, and put on her pajamas. I went back to the bathroom to clean up the crap and started crying. I could hear Emilia crying from the bathroom. Naira came over to me.

Are you sad or mad?

I'm frustrated.

What is frustrated?

Frustrated is when you want to do something, but you can't and you feel mad and sad at the same time . . .

What did you want to do?

I wanted to go hear some poems.

What is poems?

Poems . . .

I want you to go where you want to go.

APRIL 1

Emilia has started holding her hands. She is getting to know herself.

APRIL 3

There is no space for me. Ricardo tries, but he can't really be there for me. Naira asks me how I feel. Emilia is still so far from us, from this family. Maybe it's better that she stays away—away from me because I can't be there for her. Baby girl, welcome to the world. But I can't do this. I thought I could, but I can't.

APRIL 5

We are in Ecatepec. We're here to conduct interviews about violence against women. We meet with a woman named Roselia at a park bench. She watches her older children while she cradles her newborn. You, Emilia, are just a few months older. We hold our daughters and talk about her family life. She tells me her husband is a factory worker, her family needs more money, she needs to work but is scared to leave her children home alone. I ask her what she thought when she found out she was having a girl. She said that at first she felt relieved because she would finally have someone to help her with chores and look after her when she is older. But then the thought of having a daughter scared her, because this is a place where women are killed, raped, and disappeared.

"... from now on their wombs became public territory, controlled by men and the state, and procreation was directly placed at the service of capitalist accumulation." —*Caliban and the Witch* by Silvia Federici

APRIL 20

2:52 in the morning. The girls are asleep.

MAY 9

I write this after finally catching my breath. I write this because I can't allow myself to forget. Because I need to remember this in the future. Emilia spent every night last week unbearably itchy and wallowing in pain, and I thought, Why did I have another daughter. I regretted having her.

Why have another daughter. What for.

"I wanted not to give birth.... Not to be life or the source of life.... [But to be] the pillow that smothered her in her sleep. Retract the contractions by which they were both born.... Not give birth, because once they're born, motherhood is for life."
—*Empty Houses* by Brenda Navarro

A DAY IN MAY

I understand Emilia is sick. For two months, we've gone to hospitals and doctors, done treatments. But no one's been able to get rid of her eczema, which scabs over, itches, and bleeds. My mom tells me to accept it, stop fighting it, and everything will be more bearable. How can I accept this? How?

MAY 12

My relationship with Emilia is mediated by her skin condition. I don't caress her, I apply creams and ointments on her. I don't hug her, I wrap her in a bedsheet so she doesn't scratch herself. I don't kiss her cheeks, they're covered in eczema.

MAY 14

I went to my therapist, Alejandra. Actually, she's Emilia's therapist.

I tell her that I don't want to be immune to this. I don't want there to be "nothing wrong with me" as I raise my children and deal with Emilia's condition. I want to work through these things, knowing someone is there for me and I'm allowed to make mistakes.

During our session, Alejandra asks me to remember something I needed to hear from my father when I was a little girl. I stay quiet for a while and think. I can't pinpoint an exact moment, but I know I would like to have heard "Calm down, you don't have to do anything, child, you don't have to prove anything." I would have liked knowing someone was there for me. Alejandra asks me to think of a time when someone *was* there. I immediately think of Ricardo stroking my back as I breastfeed Emilia late at night. Then I think of another: Emilia lying in bed with her cracked skin, the way she looks at me and smiles as I apply ointments all over her body, without getting angry, tired, or frustrated.

I think what Emilia was trying to say is: Stay with me while I heal.

MAY 26

Jenny is the mother of Ámbar, a three-year-old girl with the same chronic condition as you. I haven't met her. We've only talked on the phone and occasionally exchange voice messages over WhatsApp, usually five to ten minutes long. The voice messages in which I'm speaking to her always end up speaking to me. Jenny reminds me that you are a girl, a baby who wants to play, interact, and be hugged. I'd forgotten that and hadn't even realized.

MAY 29

To kiss your wounds.

To kiss the pus.

To caress your broken skin.

To hug your body.

To lull you despite my fear and hopelessness. To find the words to tell you that you're going to heal and everything will be okay. To lull you with a lie.

That's why we're family.

(It's the middle of the night. Once again, your dad and I try to soothe you. He takes you to the window to distract you from the burning. I sing to you and cry.)

JULY 5

Yesterday, I scared Naira. I don't remember if I was angry or sad. I don't remember what I said to her. But she looked scared and said, "Mom, smile." Then she went over to you, Emilia, and kissed you. She lay down next to you while I applied lotions on you and said to me, "Everything is going to be okay, right?"

JULY 8

Today is my birthday.

I always wanted to be a mother.

I remember playing mom with my dolls when I was a little girl. I remember pretending to be my younger sister's mom, making her porridge and singing her lullabies. I remember my mom always happy around us, her strawberry milkshakes, and that she fed us raw eggs in orange juice every morning to make sure we ate before rushing to school. I remember camping out in our garden and the Fridays that she let us do whatever we wanted: eat with our hands, slurp our drinks, throw spitballs at each other. I remember that on our birthdays, she woke us up with snuggles and told us the story of how we were born. I remember how she would pack our bags, load us in the car, and take us somewhere—on a picnic, to a town in Michoacán or a beach in Jalisco—any chance she got. I remember she was a happy mother. If she was ever tired, scolded us, or hit us with her chancla—she must have said hurtful things—I don't remember. All I know is she was a happy mother who knew how to shape and raise happy children. I remember that even during the crisis of 1994, when her teaching salary was not enough to make ends meet, she cooked with whatever was in the pantry and made up names for each dish. My mom was a happy mom.

There's always been a lot of children in my family. My mother had six siblings and my dad had nine. Their homes were always full of children coming and going, pregnant mothers, mothers carrying children, mothers running after children. Life was about spending time with the children, at home, at parties, and sometimes at work. (I knew all the offices and schools where my mom had worked and all the janitors, secretaries, students, and colleagues there. I had an uncle who was a photographer and let us go with him to parties, another uncle who took us on field trips to watch him and his coworkers pave roads. My father took me to courthouses and assemblies in indigenous communities where he had ongoing land rights cases.)

Being a mother was a normal part of the life cycle to me. I even knew I wanted to be a mother when I was twenty-two and had a clandestine abortion at a Veracruz clinic. I knew I wanted to be a mother, just not at that moment. At the time, I was too afraid, too alone, and carrying too many dreams.

I read about the recent debates over motherhood—to be or not be a mother—online, in newspapers, and in books. I hear my friends discuss the topic and weigh in, telling them I don't recommend becoming a mother if they are not willing to give up a large part of their lives. If they are not willing to accept that they will forever have to share their freedom. I never lie to them about how exhausting it is to take care of one or two children. Or how frustrating. But is there anything worthwhile that doesn't require sleepless nights, commitment, willingness, and putting our needs aside, at times? Don't romantic relationships and friendships, for example, require all these things?

Federici writes that our body has become a public territory to feed capital. Meruane writes that children are imposed on us to force us back into our homes. But what about those of us who want to be mothers? And those of us who are working on other forms of caretaking, of taking care of ourselves?

I always wanted to be a mother.

Or rather, I never stopped to think about it.

Is the thought of being a mother thinking me?

How have we been thought? In *Por amor o por la fuerza*, Cristina Morini explains: "What makes power work, what makes us accept it, is that it doesn't act as a force that says no—instead it works through the body, produces things, provokes pleasure, shapes knowledge, produces discourse."

A DAY IN AUGUST
Emilia, you are healing, you are healing yourself. You are winning this fight, and I want to be here for every fight you put up.

AUGUST 16
Today we found a dead bird on the sidewalk.

WHILE THE GIRLS ARE ASLEEP

SEPTEMBER 2
We're on vacation visiting your aunt in Washington. Everyone in the house is sleeping, but you lay in bed, writhing in pain. A few days ago, your eczema came back along with the itching and bleeding. I have no answers. I don't know how to cure you. Someone, help me. Can anyone help me?

SEPTEMBER 13
3:54 a.m. I dance with you to reconnect with your body. To feel your body and not your condition. Dancing to save ourselves, if only for a moment.

SOME DAY IN OCTOBER
Another failed treatment.

NOVEMBER 19
The weather fucked up Emilia's skin and fucked up our second attempt at a vacation. We are back on the road, headed home.

NOVEMBER 20
I'm at home writing about parenting and both girls want to be next to me. Naira comes over with a pair of scissors to cut my hair, Emilia is crawling and then shows me she can stand up. As I write this, Naira pulls my head and Emilia crawls between my legs like a puppy.

I think of all the women who have written like this.

restricted zone: this is not your home;
at once: the followers:
          blooms.
child squatter
child skitterer
child crasher
stowaway
spore
intruder:
—*Se llaman nebulosas* by Maricela Guerrero

DECEMBER 7
"My mom is sad every morning."
"Are you sad or are you mad?"
"Mom, why are you crying?"

What memories will Naira have of me when she grows up? How will those memories shape her?

DECEMBER 21
Naira puts on her grandmother's glasses and says very seriously, "You have to take care of Emilia, but you always tell her, 'Enough, Emilia, enough.' You have to say 'Calm down,' but tell her nice, not angry. That's not smart. When you tell her angry, Emilia cries. Emilia is a baby, Emilia can't talk, she only knows how to cry. You have to tell her 'Calm down,' but tell her calm."

On days like this, I think we must be doing something right.

2018

JANUARY 9
One year. No, the second daughter wasn't easier. Yes, every daughter is different. Emilia, you arrived in the early hours of the morning full of strength and tenderness. And to teach us that raising a daughter is not about "who you want them to be," but about the person you want to be. The person you say you are.

A DAY IN FEBRUARY
Lately, what I've enjoyed most is being on flights. Especially

WHILE THE GIRLS ARE ASLEEP

long flights. This trip is transatlantic. It's the only time no one knows me, no one talks to me, no one says, "Mom, mom." I even have a routine. I take off my shoes, cover myself with a blanket, turn on the screen, click on movies, action movies, three, sometimes four in a single flight. And I ask for wine. I drink and watch like a closet drunk. I watch a documentary about a taxi driver from Ecatepec who becomes a widower and has to raise his five- or seven-year-old daughter alone. I watch *The Suffragettes*, a historical drama about the late nineteeth-century British movement for women's suffrage. I watch a movie about a teenager who hates his mother. I watch Charlize Theron, sleep-deprived, neglected, and forgotten after having her third child.

I almost always end up taking out my phone to look at photos of you two.

FEBRUARY 17

I'm at home with you girls and you both have a fever. I had to cancel all my gigs. I close the curtains and the room grows dark. I lie between you. With one hand, I caress you, Naira; you're boiling hot and breathe like a wounded bird. With the other hand, I draw circles on your back, Emilia, your little lungs working hard.

And yet, I feel good. Right here, between you, my little ones.

MARCH 20

I left the girls sleeping in bed and made myself some tea. I wanted a little time to myself to do some work. Emilia started to cry and cry and cry. Again. God, shut up already. Shut up.

Naira hid from me under the covers and started crying softly. Emilia kept crying. I joined in too. Eventually, the three of us fell asleep, exhausted.

When I woke up, I asked Naira how she had felt. She said sad because I didn't understand Emilia, that she had been crying because she's a baby, that maybe the sound my computer made when I turned it on or something outside, like an ambulance or a motorcycle, had startled her. And I didn't understand that.

But soon, it's morning again. They play and laugh together in the living room where they seem safe from me.

MARCH 22

When did I start making them feel like they're the worst thing that ever happened to me?

APRIL 2

We're home alone. I put on a lullaby and rock you to sleep. I feel all twenty pounds of you relax on my chest. In this moment, I know I can take care of you. I know you trust me.

APRIL 4

After traveling without you two these past few days, I had the space and quiet to think about some things. I realized that I'm willing to listen to stories about this country's horrors—about deaths, the disappeared, clandestine graves—but not to listen to you. To your pain, Emilia.

WHILE THE GIRLS ARE ASLEEP

APRIL 5

I remember what Carmen said to me when Naira was born:

> I made a commitment to love and care for my daughter. She is the one I share my freedom with. It sounds paradoxical, but I think it's true—a freedom you can only achieve when you let go.

APRIL 6

Not all of us are parents, but we've all been children, we've all been cared for.

APRIL 7

To care for another is exhausting. Care is overwhelming. Devastating.

SOME DAY IN APRIL OR MAY

Emilia: I'm not sure what's changed, but you're here. I mean that you're here, with me, that we are together. I am your mother and you are my daughter. It took me so long to realize that your skin condition hurts you (I was too focused on my frustration); it took me so long to realize that looking at books cures your insomnia, kissing your cheeks puts you to sleep, and hiding toys from your sister amuses you.

MAY 20

At 9:16 p.m., the earthquake alarm started blaring. The girls were asleep, and I was reading in my pajamas. Ricardo was still at work. I grabbed Naira and threw her over my shoulder, then Emilia. I walked to the door but couldn't open it with my hands full. I put Naira down, told her to wake up and help me, but she was wobbling. I opened the door and threw her back over my shoulder. I rushed down three flights of stairs as fast as I could with fifty pounds of dead weight on me. The neighbors were already downstairs. They opened the door for me, took the girls, and put a jacket on them.

They wrapped me in a blanket or towel, I don't really remember.

I think that's a good metaphor for motherhood: fifty pounds of dead weight on me.

JULY 7
Time. What is it that happens while I brush their hair before bed?

AUGUST 2
We have to leave early to take Emilia to the doctor. Naira wants to bring seven toys to school, and I tell her she can't take so many, she needs to pick three. But she wants all seven: a kitty, another kitty, a puppy, a pony, another pony, a doll, and her music box. Naira ignores me. I raise my voice. She insists. I throw her toys on the floor. Naira cries. I ignore her.

Thirty minutes later, I get an email:

Dear authors and allies,
I'm writing to say hello and remind you about the upcoming deadline to submit to our anthology. I hope

you're putting the final touches on your pieces. I look forward to reading them!

I haven't even started yet.

AUGUST 3
It's not you, little one. I'm just tired, stressed, behind on work.

AUGUST 9
How do we return to love?

AUGUST 11
I go through my diary and realize just how many times you have saved me, Naira.

My friend and I think through it together. She tells me that after those delirious moments when she wants to get rid of her son, she looks into his eyes. But what I need in those moments is some space and silence. Then the girls bring me back. Sometimes, they come over to hug my legs, other times they say, "Mama, are you sad or mad?" Or Naira stays in bed, hiding under the covers, until she falls asleep. And just like that, when she doesn't demand anything from me, I can come back to them.

AUGUST 12
Things I know are true:

Having a child is a selfish choice—it's to choose for someone to be born and exist. Giving in to our selfishness means we must commit to taking care of them.

We don't love our daughters just because they are our daughters. We learn to love them. Or not.

AUGUST 16
I show a draft of this text to a feminist friend. It makes her uncomfortable that I use the words "shame" and "ashamed."

She insists (she's told me many times) that shame and guilt are patriarchal burdens that don't belong to me. I tell her that I don't understand why it makes her uncomfortable. When I feel ashamed, I'm not thinking about what people will say. I'm thinking about my daughters and what they experience because our relationship shapes them—it shapes us. By talking about those feelings of shame, they stop being only mine, as if I swept them out of our house.

AUGUST 18

I go through the diary I've kept for four years, deleting the days that seem too cheesy or that I don't think I'm ready to share. Why and for whom did I write this diary? Maybe for them, in case they're ever curious or ask about their birth. Maybe for myself, so I don't feel alone. Maybe so they don't feel alone someday. Maybe so they can be a bit more free. So we can all be a bit more free.

Cristina Rivera Garza
tr. Heather Cleary

FIRST PERSON PLURAL

1. SPORADIC COMMUNITIES

I returned to Mexico in 2003 after spending nearly fifteen years in the United States. I had published a few novels by then, which might have been why certain newspapers occasionally asked me to share my thoughts. This time, the topic was Cortázar. Apparently, it's essential to ask readers their opinion of Cortázar every year. And every year, those readers reaffirm their admiration for a body of work that unfurls itself time and again before new eyes. When it was my turn, however, I said that I didn't like the character of La Maga and that *Hopscotch*, the elastic, performative novel that Cortázar published on June 28, 1963, hadn't aged well, especially regarding gender. My answer was limited to a certain number of characters, including spaces, so instead of explaining my position with quotations from the novel and theoretical frameworks, I simply gave my opinion. The response was immediate. One critic, in the column he wrote for a national paper at the time, told me to shut up. "Wouldn't we all be better off if Cris just shut up?" he mused, after making it clear that he disagreed with my reading of Cortázar and citing Steiner, when I had mentioned Stein. Gertrude Stein. In the early years of the twenty-first century, a professional critic I had never met was abridging my name in that fake tone of intimacy so often employed to belittle one's interlocutor. This was Mexico, in the spring of 2004. That kind of thing passed for normal.

When I asked other writers and acquaintances how to respond to something like that, an aggression on that scale, most agreed that the best idea was not to say anything. What did I expect, insulting a writer venerated by generations? Didn't I know what happened to those who strayed from the doctrine? You can't mess with Cortázar and not expect consequences, they whispered ruefully. But others, many others, took it upon themselves to write intelligent, informed responses that I posted one by one on the blog I kept at the time. It was called *No hay tal lugar*—contemporary utopics. Those who responded, those who invested time and energy in contributing to a debate I considered urgently important in a country where the femicide machine was endlessly marking women's bodies with the blades of its violence, were writers and professors, bloggers and freelancers, foreigners, readers. Thanks to them, thanks to their company and their companionship, I was able to write a relatively clear and calm response. Thanks to them, instead of shutting up as instructed, I was able to write.

From near and far, reacting immediately to the event as it unfolded, these women and men brought their words together to form a small, sporadic community that dispersed again after completing its mission. Sporadic is an adjective that denotes something that happens occasionally, without clear precursors or continuations. But sporadic, which comes from the Medieval Latin *sporadicus*, which comes from the Greek *sporadikos*, also means "scattered." *Sporas* means "seed" or "a sowing" in Greek. According to the Oxford dictionary, in biology, a spore is "a minute, typically one-celled, reproductive unit capable of giving rise to a new individual without sexual fusion," and also "a rounded resistant form adopted by a bacterial cell in adverse conditions." We do have something in common with single-celled organisms when we come together briefly to spread and survive; when, after long periods of apparent dormancy, we overcome adverse conditions and emerge at a precise moment for seconds or hours or days, then continue along our respective paths. We have something in common with spores when we disperse. And also when, thanks to memory, we return and persist and re-write.

In 2004, when the Mexican literary establishment's hegemonic patriarchy declared it perfectly normal to belittle a woman and tell her to shut up because its members disagreed with her, a sporadic community of scribes said otherwise. That small but courageous act turned into a conversation and a closeness that has evolved in vastly different ways over the years. Several friends from those days have turned into irritating enemies. Others have remained in touch, reaching out from train stations and waiting rooms. I've lost contact with some. I even ended up talking with the critic who had tried to silence me, out of the public sphere, over little sips of whiskey in his home. The violence against women remains unchanged, it is true, but all these years later—now that silence is no longer the normal or expected response to either micro or colossal acts of violence—I find myself thinking about the myriad sporadic gatherings that gradually spread their small truths throughout the air we breathe. Things don't change from one day to the next, but the limits of the tolerable are reduced or realigned the more we talk about them within our circles. The more we talk beyond our circles about the pain they cause.

2. ROOMS OF ONE'S OTHER[1]

Rebecca Solnit is right to remind us that when Virginia Woolf wrote about that now-famous room of one's own, she was not advocating for a lofty ivory tower that would separate her from the world, but rather a world in which equal pay and access to education, especially at the university level, would afford women the resources necessary to carve out time and space to do their work. In this sense, a room of one's own was actually a room for every woman. Or to be more exact: a time and space made possible by the many people around us.

We live in societies that celebrate independence to an extraordinary degree. One of capitalism's foundational myths is that of the self-made man, who—thanks to his pluck and tenacity—overcomes all obstacles and becomes his own private god. Never mind that all members of our species need material and emotional care for a long time after we're born, or that later—social beings that we are—we depend on language and affective bonds in order to walk the face of the earth in the company of others. We are with others, there's no way around it. Moreover, we depend on others. Though contemporary therapy has turned this foundational interdependence into a mere pathology, something one might overcome with a dose of self-esteem and discipline, it's good to remember that no one can have a room of their own without a house, without

---

1. Translator's note: The title of this section, "Habitaciones impropias," is a play on the translation into Spanish of Virginia Woolf's *A Room of One's Own* as *Una habitación propia.* "Impropia," however, also carries the meaning of something that is improper, inappropriate, strange, or out of place. We should keep this sense in mind as we read because not only is Rivera Garza writing against an individualistic understanding of the room of one's own, she is also positing the recognition of interdependence as a transgressive act.

a community around and inside that house, constituting and affecting it. Indeed, we must not forget that the existence of a room of one's own depends entirely on the existence of materials for its construction and skilled laborers to put those materials together in the right way. We are forever in debt to the human and nonhuman elements that offer us shelter. As a result, every room is, in effect, a room of one's other, including the one Virginia Woolf proposed. It is a grace afforded us by the wishes and kindnesses of so many others. Strictly speaking, it is a space loaned to us. All we get is the right to use it.

It usually takes a lifetime to find or build those rooms of and toward one's other. Often, we need to leave behind houses taken over by invisible (read: normalized) patriarchal forces, those spaces where inequality is structural and silence is the cement that holds everything in place. This house could literally be your paternal home, but it could also be the classroom or the office or a cubicle at the library. Whatever name it bears, whatever form it takes, we must say goodbye to all that and confront a world where—surprising no one—those same strategies of domination are repeated over and over. It doesn't take long to realize that what lies outside the workplace or domestic sphere isn't the opposite of what's inside, but rather its continuation by different means. Its confirmation. This is why, for me, it's always been about how to escape. I don't know where I learned it, but one of my first life lessons was this: as soon as I entered any room, I should locate the exit—the door through which my body could pass, when the time came, in search of something else.

According to Dimitris Papadopoulos, people don't escape *from*; people escape. Escape is the original movement. First there was nomadism and later, by force of control or scarcity or fear, came sedentary life. The building of roofs. Walls.

Windows. If this is true, and I do think it is, it's not enough to open the door and go out in search of those rooms. We must also understand that any room we pass through is fleeting. Important, but temporary. I have lived in modest rooms filled with books, comfortable rooms with carpets and large windows, rooms in *vecindades* with concrete floors and a musty odor, rooms with a view of the sea. In the beginning, when I was in a terrible rush and the future seemed bigger than the past, I tried never to leave a trace. It would never have crossed my mind to write "Cristina was here" anywhere. I was trying to make myself invisible so I could escape the nebulous blades of power. I was trying to run faster, react more nimbly. I was trying not to have a body (which might be why I forgot to eat). My body, like that room, tied me inevitably and unrelentingly to narratives that, although I understood them, did not move me.

Simone de Beauvoir was right: one is not born, but rather becomes, a woman. Which is to say, one is made into a woman. With the passing of time, as the terrors of my teenage years have taken on names and specific contours, I have grown less resistant to leaving signs of myself. I know we are legion. Along my paths I met other women who, like me, barreled forward, guided more by a raging survival instinct than by the desire to achieve any concrete goal. Forget about hope. There was no time for that. We were trying to save our hides, literally. In the animated video "The End of Carrying it All," the artist Wangechi Mutu depicts a woman who carries an entire world on her head as she walks the furthest reaches of the earth. Though Mutu has explained that, like the civilization it interpellates and condemns, the load carried by the woman is heavy because she has accumulated more than she should have, it is also possible to see this figure as a body carrying its home on its back. A shimmering snail. A being unto itself. Certain things could be left behind, like oil wells or buildings that take more than they give, but not birds. In the animation, the weight is so overwhelming that the woman ends up being swallowed by the earth. And, ultimately, who isn't? After watching the images for a long time, I wonder if they're more an allegory of autonomy than a warning about our complicity with the earth's enemies. But the end of carrying it all is also a beginning: beginning to carry just a little. Of carrying only what is necessary, only what allows for a light step, for lighter friendships. I always used to dream of a long, rectangular table at which everyone had a seat. Now I dream of a three-dimensional origami version of that table that I can carry, delicately folded, tucked into my bra. With me always.

3. AGAINST LOVE

I can still see them in the distance. There they go, crossing the street on a covered pedestrian overpass. They are talking nonstop. If I could hear them from where I am, I would know they are writing a poem together, line by line. They agree: love is a trap. Their first collaborative piece will be this poem against love. Up there, before they descend the metal stairs but already surrounded by the strident noises of the city, they kiss. Above them, the leaden gray of factories and sparse clouds.

I was always suspicious of love. I watched as friends I had seen as talented, voracious women knelt with staggering frequency at the altar of love. One day, they were talking about how they wanted to climb the Alps or visit the Great Wall of China or write the Great Mexican Novel, and the next, apparently out of nowhere, they were caught in the net of a narrative for which they were willing to trade their whole lives, including—or especially—their dreams. It was easy to draw hasty conclusions from all this: love was the real enemy. A woman shouldn't fall in love if she wanted to make her plans and desires a reality. She needed to protect her heart and be selective in how she attended to the call of her body. One of my favorite tactics during that period was to fall madly in love with people beyond my reach for one reason or another, people I didn't know well and with whom I had only the slightest, most tentative contact. In that way, I maintained the theatricality of love, the nerves and intensity that we ascribe to it, but from the safe distance offered by correspondence. Another tactic was to share my body but keep all the rest under lock and key: books, ideas, plans for the future. My writing.

Back then, I thought love was the enemy—any kind of love, not just the kind invented by capitalism and heteropatriarchy to dominate a large part of the population. That kind of love, which horrified me and from which I fled in ways I'm only now beginning to unpack, contained a large dose of the famed romantic love, but it was also seasoned with a division of labor in which the work of care and reproduction just happened to fall to the woman, within and outside the space of the home. As Silvia Federici has observed, this invisible, endless, unpaid labor is the very foundation of the perverse dynamics of love in the time of late neoliberalism. Where my besotted friends saw everlasting bonds and destinies fulfilled, my teenage self glimpsed a vague but threatening landscape of prisons, exploitation, disgrace.

One of the strategies employed by the poet Claudia Rankine in *Citizen*, a book that takes a stand against the burgeoning racism that pervades the United States, and which has consolidated her reputation as one of the most profound thinkers working in English today, is the clear and concrete description of situations that power has actively sought to render ambiguous. Time and again, faced with scenes that lend themselves to misunderstanding, the poetic voice asks itself and us: "Did he really just say that?" And the answer, complex but empirical, written in the grays of a reality that is never univocal, but which can be clearly identified, is: yes. Yes, this is discrimination. This is called racism. This is clearly unequal treatment. The reader cannot close *Citizen* without knowing beyond the shadow of a doubt that many of the situations they had never dared to describe as such were, in fact, racist. What Rankine's poetry offers the reader is a firm and measured, definitely clear-eyed companionship in the process of recognizing the injustice and violence of many different situations that, at the time, other people tried to pass off as something else. The gift Rankine offers us is the grace of the word that liberates in the moment of naming.

What Rankine did to draw back the curtain on racism, the writing of Simone de Beauvoir and Rosario Castellanos did with respect to heterosexual love. I owe to the former a phrase that I would have liked to tattoo somewhere visible on my right arm: "On the day when it will be possible for woman to love not in her weakness but in her strength, not to escape herself but to find herself, not to abase herself but to assert herself—on that day love will become for her, as it is for man, a source of life and not of mortal danger." The latter has left me with countless poems in which love's wound is accompanied by devastating, unsentimental explorations about the uneven conditions between lovers. In "Agony Outside the Wall," Castellanos writes: "Stay away from me, man who makes the world / Let me be, there is no need to kill me." In "False Elegy": "All we share is a slow calamity. / I see myself die in you, in another, in everything. / And still I yawn or let my mind wander / As if watching a dull performance." Finally, these lines from "Meditation on the Threshold," which are cited even more often: "There must be another way, one that isn't called Sappho / or Messalina or Mary of Egypt / or Magdalene or Clémence Isaure, / another way to be human and free. / Another way to be." Precisely. Another way to be. Today, we would need to add: another way that isn't called Rosario Castellanos, or Elena Garro, or Inés Arredondo. Another way to be human and free.

But the brutality of unequal love doesn't only affect women. Love has rarely been more terrifying than in the hands of a man named Karl Ove Knausgaard, who—not because he is deeply in love, or perhaps precisely because he is—sets aside his merciless powers of observation in the second volume of his long autobiographical project, *My Struggle*. Because his aim is not to write fiction, or even strictly to tell a story, but rather to approach the nucleus of life, his writing quickly diverges from both the stereotypical tales of mad love that character- ize so many twentieth-century books and the many erudite treatises, including one penned by Alain Badiou, that cele- brate—in fairly abstract terms—lasting, committed, mature love. Sticking close to bodies and objects, never straying from direct observation but also never worrying where that gaze moves or what it confirms, Knausgaard's descriptions manage to touch upon what it means to love in the early twenty-first century as a member of the urban intellectual middle class. Be warned: it's not pretty. It is powerful, but not pretty in the way bedtime stories are pretty. That is, in the way fiction is pretty. The protagonists of this love and this truth, Karl Ove and Linda, didn't live "happily ever after," but they were happy, yes. Tentatively and intermittently, often without planning it or realizing it—and, frankly, in spite of themselves.

Faithful to the principles established in the first volume of his autobiography, Knausgaard holds nothing back from the reader of this love story. Covering the sublime moments of their encounter and the dramas of their conflicts with the same minute attention, the Knausgaardian gaze lingers with unique prowess on the material aspects of a shared life: the division of domestic labors and the disputes over free time, the relationship between activities in the home and salaried work. Indeed, much of this love story focuses on the labor of purchasing and preparing food, washing clothes, cleaning the kitchen and the bedroom, tending to the children. Who does what and for how long is perhaps the most frequent topic of conversation between these lovers, who, often exhausted if not outright annoyed, rush to defend with tooth and nail the little free time they have. "[Should we] ignore an important part of a great poet and diarist's life for the sake of decency? Forget the unpleasantness?" Knausgaard asks rhetorically before advancing through the plethora of annoying, thankless, unkind, and often boring details that make up the life of a couple in love.

These are not the elements most often associated with romantic love, or even with filial love, now being explored by certain Latin American novels increasingly alert to gender differences and hierarchies, but they are the conditions of a love that is real, substantial, and thousands of times renewed. It is not only happy in the way of stories, but it is. It is not only wretched in the way of impossibility, but it is. The next time you wish for true love, you should really stop and think. And, at the same time, take Rosario Castellanos's words to heart and assume the task of creating, with others, that other way to be human and free. I think of the long and loving letter that Gabriela Wiener wrote to her mother to explain her unusual sentimental arrangement, which had grown into a threesome that fundamentally discredits the egotistical, voracious principles of capital, and I say to myself: Here we go. Another way to be. I would like to think that her letter is, in this moment, reaching those teenagers on the urban bridge, who loved each other the way one loves that city—furiously. Better late than never.

4. THE FEMINIST'S REPOSE

Sara Ahmed has said that living a feminist life means turning everything into a question. And by everything she means, precisely, everything. The floor across which we drag our feet; the bodies we inhabit; the families we come from and those we form in turn; the structures of class and race that so determine our daily experiences; the public spaces to which we do or do not have access; the domestic sphere; the way we care for one another, and the many ways we fail to do so; how we approach others and how we withdraw when we need silence and privacy. A feminist lives with eyes wide open. To be a feminist, Ahmed insists, you must always be a student. Feminist movements occupy the public sphere, but they can also happen when a woman says "enough," alone in a room that will no longer hold her. If all this is true, and I'm certain that it is, when do feminists rest?

Much has been said about the warrior's repose, that mythical image of the home to which, having completed his tasks, the man returns in search of care, food, sex. The patriarchal dimension of the phrase is hardly subtle. When the warrior tires of his exploits in the public sphere, he returns to the domestic realm, where—thanks to the immutable hierarchy that exists there—he can relax and recover his strength for his next adventure. We know little about the thoughts and feelings of the home's other inhabitants, since their function in this inflexible story is basically just to welcome him back and provide services and care with a cheery demeanor, if not with gratitude. How did they manage to survive during the warrior's long absence? How did they get water, firewood, food? Did they ever allow themselves to feel the effects of that distant war that was nonetheless within reach in that mythical home, since the warrior does return? The phrase itself tells us not to think about that. They managed, somehow. We feminist killjoys shouldn't go around asking impossible questions! What matters is the warrior's happiness, his rest. What matters is that the image of the home remains immaculate, a Romantic painting unassailed by the question of accumulation. But here I am again, in the act of questioning, when I had meant to talk about repose.

A few years ago, while reading a profile of the famous feminist Gloria Steinem, I was surprised by the activist's confession that, after years of ignoring her private life, she had finally realized that she needed time for herself. Looking back, she saw only stacks of still-unopened boxes in messy rooms where she rarely, if ever, sat down to eat. Years later, Gloria finally wanted her repose. I was struck by a similar surprise as I nosed around in Gloria Anzaldúa's personal papers in the Benson Collection at the University of Texas–Austin. In addition to many of the drawings she used in her workshops and classes, the archive contains detailed lists of what she ate every day. For example, though she already knew she suffered from diabetes, one less-than-healthy night the borderland feminist ate four tamales. Mindful of the fluctuations in her spiritual life, she also kept recordings of her tarot readings and other metaphysical explorations. These small pieces of her private life are moving because at a moment when it was critical to emphasize woman's entry into the public sphere, much of the complexity found in the home and its private aura remained hidden.

Complex and sometimes contradictory, these women not only taught us to move through life with our eyes open, questioning everything, but also to seek shelter in everyday spaces, in collective spaces, when exhaustion, health, or simple preference demands it. Though it is possible to talk about many different forms of feminism, it is also possible to say that all of them, with their dissonances and their assonances, agree on the political and vital importance of the body. This is why these and so many other feminists have also needed to dedicate time to the body at rest. "Always drink a glass of water after bathing," insisted my grandmother, who never called herself a feminist, though she was one. I remember that piece of advice, along with many others that came to shape how I move through the world. It was unexpected encounters along my escape routes that connected me with other fugitive women and the awareness that my solitude had come to an end, but my first-person plural has only continued to grow. It is present in the letters I string together on this screen, since together we construct a language. It is in the hands that harvested the tea I drink, and those that made the cup and plate that bring it first to my lips, and then into my body. Just as with every object that makes this text possible: the computer, the table, the chair, the window. According to the poet Fred Moten, there are no soloists—there is only accompaniment. Living a feminist life today is feeling that fact in every one of our bones.

Diana J. Torres
tr. Heather Cleary

MEDAL OR STIGMA

I'M WRITING THIS text five days after being stabbed in the street for the first time. I spent the whole first day in the emergency room of Mexico City's General Hospital, where I realized that public hospitals are the same everywhere.

The next three days were gray—both outside the building and inside me. Sleeping all day, waking up to take my painkillers, poisoning myself with antibiotics, healing my wound, watching series, watching movies, eating, receiving love: doing only what helped to dispel the storm clouds, or to ignore them altogether. And now, on my fifth day with this wound, I'm finally beginning to think about what happened; to remember, to analyze. I don't know if it's the medicine I've had, or the alcohol I haven't (I'm currently on my longest dry streak since the time I had appendicitis), or the pain that comes at times, but my mind is clearer than usual. I guess that's why I'm writing.

Thoughts, images, and memories: the mugger's voice and the glint of his blade, the face of the woman who was with me, the fear in all our eyes, my refusal to be mugged because what I was carrying was too valuable to just hand it over to some kid with a knife.

His attempt to get close to my body, my bag hitting his face, his blow to my leg, his escape. The heat of the blood streaming toward my foot and pooling in my boot, the realization that I had been stabbed, my fat poking through the hole, the angled fibers in the depths of the reddest red, the lights, the looks, the passivity of the witnesses—the horrible response that is the lack of response. The truth is that none of it matters, and what matters even less: the color of the kid's skin; what time we went to the Oxxo for cigarettes; the substances running through our veins—all of us—that night. In this case, only gender matters.

It's all my little brain (which compulsively tries to explain every damn thing) has been able to latch onto to keep me entertained for a few hours during my convalescence, which, for someone like me who can't sit still, has been pretty tedious.

I've been going out at all hours of the night for five years now, walking the deserted streets guided by my three elemental drives: cold beer, cigarettes, and making my partner happy; she once told me that she fell in love with me because I'm always ready to brave a beer run, whatever time it is, whatever state I'm in. That's because I love the streets when they're all mine (or seem to be), and I've always experienced that as one of the clearest victories of feminism. But even though the streets are indeed ours, that statement has too many unsaid *ifs* attached to it when you're a woman—even more so if you're a woman who looks like one, which is not my case. It's a power I acquired when I arrived in Mexico City; ironically, I feel much safer here than I did in Barcelona, where the fear of being arrested descended on me whenever I left the house.

Nothing out of this world had ever happened during my nocturnal adventures, except a few encounters with harmless drunks and the occasional driver who would pull his car over to proposition me, thinking I was a male sex worker; then there was that time three guys chased me down the street, dead set on beating the shit out of me, screaming "fucking faggot!" because I was in a miniskirt and had painted my nails. And I'm not

MEDAL OR STIGMA

talking about just any city (that might matter too, that thing called geopolitics): I'm talking about Mexico City, mainly in Obrera and Doctores, the two neighborhoods where I've always lived and worked, and which—though I never experienced the violence, myself—seem to be two of the most complicated parts of the city.

This kind of immunity, which very few women can enjoy as I do, is clearly tied to my appearance—I guess because I don't look like a woman or a man, or even your average teen: my hair, my face, my tattoos, and probably a lot of other details make me someone who isn't particularly "muggable," much less "rapeable."

Unfortunately, and to contradict the popular saying, not all cats are black in the night. Practically every one of my friends has been assaulted (sexually or otherwise) on those nighttime streets that I walk in relative peace.

Considering all the terrible things that can happen to a woman walking the streets of Mexico City alone (or accompanied by another woman), I think I got off easy—not because I'm not a woman, but because other people don't read me as one, and also because, after the fact, what happened to me is seen as something between heroic and stupid, rather than horrific or shameful. The people who called me brave or silly for not just letting myself be mugged, or who called my wound a "battle scar," would have reacted very differently if I had been raped or beaten to a pulp. No one sees me as a victim.

Meanwhile, the kid who stabbed me probably thought I was another guy, an equal—despite being white and strange-looking—who might have something worth stealing; he ran off terrified when I defended myself, even if he did put a hole in my leg.

A friend comes to visit me in the afternoon. She brings cigarettes and affection. And it's only when I tell her what happened that I realize it wasn't just a robbery, and that my wound isn't just a wound.

There is, in fact, something bigger behind all this; there are many questions, and maybe also a few answers. If we're going to talk about violence and privilege here, in Mexico, in this country that has become a pool of blood, it would be deeply dishonest to simplify things and let these events pass as insignificant.

I feel that those of us who have the privilege to be able to reflect on what happens around us also have a kind of obligation to try to make our reflections serve collective knowledge and understanding, so that what we've gone through can be useful in some way. It's our responsibility to think and to speak out, because the vast majority of people who suffer this violence every day—on levels we can't even imagine—are silenced by the system itself, which is entirely complicit in this whole shitshow.

We talk, and I tell her that having been stabbed is really weird because even though my leg has an inch-long hole in it and the fibers of my quadriceps are stitched together just like my skin, and it's fucking painful and difficult to move around, my emotions remain in one piece.

In fact, I feel remarkably good on an emotional level, and that's the strange thing. My friend and I talk about how dangerous the streets are in the city we live in, but do not belong to, since we're both from somewhere else; we also talk about everyday violence. I know she's harassed on the street every day—those terribly named "catcalls" or ass-grabbing on a crowded subway car, all that crap. But she doesn't mention any of it because there's no need: we both know what we mean when we talk about violence.

When she leaves, I start thinking about all my loved ones who have been violated and humiliated, and they all have one

MEDAL OR STIGMA 275

thing in common: they're all femme women or queer men. Obviously, many of my masculine male friends have experienced violent incidents in their lives, but these incidents are usually either at the hands of law enforcement or in fights with other machos over a girl or whatever machos fight about, and they're never something the men wish hadn't happened— on the contrary, they're proud of these events and construct their masculinity around them, adding them to their lists of achievements. Being involved in physical confrontations with other men is actually something they tend to brag about. I can't imagine a woman bragging about how many times she's been sexually assaulted, can you?

If violence is something that leaves wounds or traces, or whatever we want to call them, we should recognize that, for people of all genders, those wounds either act as medals (the hero showing off battle scars) or become stigmata. And by "stigmata," I mean marks that prevent someone from living without fear, from living with some small measure of happiness and peace of mind; I mean marks that turn a person into a victim.

It is here, then, in the consequences or outcomes of experiencing a violent act, where I think the greatest divergence exists between how feminized and masculinized bodies are affected, which is merely a symptom of the social rot many of us call the patriarchy, a system that makes even something bad into something less bad for the quintessentially privileged: men (and those of us who are read as such). I honestly have no idea how to change all this, though it might help a lot if there were a change in the general attitude toward aggressions of all types and, above all, toward their so-called victims.

When men criticize feminism—claiming that it ignores or bypasses the death and suffering they expose themselves to by going to war or defending women in the street (from the attack of another man)—or when they talk about how hard it is to grow up not being allowed to cry or be sensitive or any of that other bullshit, their thinking is shaped completely by the way they understand violence as something common and unavoidable, that is, as something normal and even desirable, something they themselves foster and revere like a deity because one of the things that make them "men" is, precisely, their ability to face it, to create it, to turn it into their favorite plaything.

And so, one of the aftereffects of experiencing an act of violence—from my masculinized perspective—is the absence of fear and the empowerment that comes from that. That's how I've been feeling: empowered. Maybe because I poured a good quantity of my blood into the jaws of this monstrous city as an offering, I feel like we're somehow even, and that gives me a sense of protection. Sometimes things frighten us more in our imaginations than when they really happen; if you had told me a week ago that I was going to be stabbed during a robbery, I probably would've shat myself, even though right now I don't see it as something to be scared of. Right now, I see it as an experience I needed to face, one which had the power to make me stronger.

Of all the many horrible things that could happen to a woman walking alone, the fact that being raped is considered, both collectively and individually, to be much worse than being stabbed is not an objective assessment, it's a cultural one. In both situations, another person (or several) inflict damage to our body in a nonconsensual way by introducing into it something that injures us and will leave a scar. The big problem lies in the reading we and others make of these aggressions, in the way we face the things that shouldn't happen to us but do. I

MEDAL OR STIGMA

think that, since we can't put an end to violence, it is our collective responsibility to change that perception.

I'm not sure I know how to make this change, but I think we shouldn't wait until someone fucks with us, and that maybe we should start putting this issue on the agenda, since our various feminisms talk a lot about how to deal with gender-based aggressions, but we don't really talk about how to keep our scars from becoming stigmas, much less about strategies we might use to develop the "immunity" that has given me such freedom and peace of mind, and which I don't think is only a question of how I look, but also a result of how much I listen to my intuition, my connection to things we can't see (the divine, or energies), and maybe also my race and education, though those aren't things I chose.

I'm convinced that women have been stripped of our intuition and our connection with the divine, among other things, in order to make us more vulnerable; I also believe that it's up to us to restore that connection.

The suspicion that something more than just my appearance has protected me all this time has been growing inside me all day. I don't really know how to describe it, but on those nocturnal walks of mine, I never really feel "alone" because I'm always surrounded by something like a crew of protective beings I sometimes call deities, and to whom I dedicate a lot of thought and care—though not as much lately because I've been working nonstop.

But today, when I'm thinking like I haven't in ages, another thing that I keep wondering about—though I've tried hard to ignore the idea because it sounds too surreal, even to me—is whether what happened to me had anything to do with the scapular of the Virgin of Juquila I tore from my neck while dancing up a storm in Playa Vicente almost two months ago. Since then, it's been one awful thing after another: one of the revelers that night died when a wall fell on him at the construction site where he was working (rest in peace, lovely Brayan), the bloodthirsty ticks that are the government and its minions sucking the life from my humble business venture (La Cañita, stop by any time), the armed robbery of the aforementioned business (though I prefer that kind of stealing to the bureaucratic version), the theft of my only mode of transportation—my beloved bicycle—and my cell phone (I'm growing accustomed to its absence, for better or worse), and a number of other small tragedies that were completely eclipsed by the real ones. The question of how all this connects to a Virgin of Juquila angry with me for tearing off her beautiful necklace in a moment of rapture is rattling around in my head and, unfortunately, I don't have an answer.

What I do know is that I carried some kind of amulet around with me for protection since I arrived in Mexico, and in the weeks I've gone through life "unprotected," all sorts of things have happened to me—the most radical of which was, of course, seeing my mortality up close: that knife could easily have entered my body a few inches over and severed my femoral artery, or a bit higher up and pierced my heart.

This might all sound like nonsense, like it has nothing to do with what I was talking about, but I think one of the things that kept me safe in the streets until now, aside from my masculinity, is my spirituality—how I endow objects with the ability to watch over me or to connect me with whatever I believe watches over me.

I think that what matters most isn't how we experience violence, but rather what we do with it in a society where it seems inevitable, or even better, how we might transform and avoid it. I'm not suggesting that one way to prevent rape is for women to stop looking like women, because one way or another they'd be suffering some kind of aggression like what I experienced five days ago, and anyway, it's another form of violence that we can't go out dressed however we want, whenever we want. Or that we should all go around with scapulars around our necks and imploring the gender-nonspecific deities to protect us.

I believe that a good step forward might be refusing to normalize the violent acts that tear through us, refusing to view them as a defeat and thinking instead of ways to transform them, from the privileged position of being able to reflect and talk and write about them. In fact, many people here in Mexico are already doing precisely that, especially from feminist perspectives. I'm just joining in because I don't want to be a victim. I don't want to carry a stigma.

Sara Uribe
tr. Heather Cleary

ALONE

OF ALL THE times my father beat me when I was a child, I only really remember one. It was a Sunday afternoon; I was seven, doing my homework in the living room. He was whistling and it distracted me, so I asked him to stop. His rage was always spontaneous combustion: the minute I saw him stand, I ran into the bedroom and locked the door. What hurt most, what I was most sorry about that day, was that I had asked him to be quiet so I could focus. I was full of remorse, not because I cared all that much about getting beaten, but because the body he eventually unleashed his fury on was not mine. My father, searching for the key. My father, in the hallway. My father, opening the door. I hid in the closet, searching in vain for protection. When he raised his heavy arm, my mother slid between us. She was the one who paid the price for the audacity of a little girl asking for quiet, of a woman silencing a man.

One Saturday morning a few months later, as we were watching a Tin Tan movie, my mother asked me and my sister, who was barely two years older than me, if we wanted our father to move out. I don't want to make this decision alone, she said; I want to know what you want. The response was unanimous. And that was how I watched my father—out of the corner of my eye, because the movie was awesome and I didn't want to miss anything—walk out of our lives with a brown suitcase in his hand. He couldn't have had much to do with us if that one little bag could hold his part of the life we had shared. My mother told us to say goodbye. I gave him a hurried, indifferent hug out front, as if in that moment I realized nothing bound me to him anymore, that the blood ties that had supposedly made us father and daughter—family— were broken, empty, meaningless.

My mother died in 1989. Rheumatoid arthritis took over her ailing fifty-five-year-old body and laid it out, first in her bed and eventually in a coffin. She was keenly aware how little time she had left: that was why she moved us from Querétaro to Ciudad Valles in San Luis Potosí, and why she decided on her brother as the best option to care for her daughters. The last two times I saw my father was at my mother's funeral and when he came looking for us because he was filling out paperwork for his retirement: he would get a bigger pension for each child he could claim.

Life with my uncle was not as my mother had planned it. He was a violent man too. I remember his blows, his surveillance, his intimidation: no television, no radio, no going out. Come to think of it, Fernando practically held us captive for a whole year in the house where our mother died. We were only allowed out to go to class. I was in high school, and my sister went to a secretarial academy. Fernando made it very clear: our destiny was to become receptionists or shop girls.

One time we snuck out to go to a local fair, and Fernando caught us. That was when he sent us to boarding school in León, Guanajuato. He forced us to sign a document stating that we agreed to be locked up there for a year. I say "locked up" because the place was more like a juvenile detention center than a boarding school, with its long halls lined with beds covered in blankets—white with black stripes—meant to look like the bars that held in fifty women between the ages of twelve and thirty-five.

I don't know where we found the rebellious streak to get ourselves expelled. Mute with rage, Fernando picked us up at the boarding school only to take us to the station in León and put us on a bus back to Ciudad Valles. I watched him standing there on the curb as we pulled out, not knowing that we'd never hear his voice again, that we'd never again be intimidated by his anger, his punishments, or his prohibitions. Not knowing that, just a week later, a heart attack would excise him from the plot of our lives.

At fourteen and twelve years old, my sister and I were left without a legal guardian and began to live on the margin of the state. By law, as minors, we should have been someone's wards. In the absence of such a person, we were supposed to be sent to an orphanage or one of the girls' homes set up by the DIF, the national system of child welfare and family services. Since the house my mother left us was right across the street from Fernando's, our neighbors and everyone around us thought that his wife, Lupe, had taken us as her wards. But no. No parent, no guardian, no state.

We lied constantly. We invented a guardian, forged signatures. We found someone willing to pretend they were a relative in charge of our care. That's how we got by until we turned eighteen.

At some point during those years, Lupe gave us a stack of documents Fernando had left in his office. That was also when she told us she'd wanted to leave my uncle and had asked him for a divorce not long before he died. He went crazy, she said, and pulled a gun out of who-knows-where. He got on his knees and told her he would kill himself right then and there if she left him. He held the gun to his temple, she said.

The documents resurfaced a few years ago, during my last move. I needed to read one of them several times before I understood what wasn't being said. Before I realized what it actually meant. It was the state asking the state to return two minors to the custody and protection of the man who had tried to kill their mother—in other words, their father.

```
DIF
89-91
LOCAL COMMITTEE
CD. VALLES S. L. P.

September 8, 1990

DR. GERMAN GAYTAN GAMBOA
DIRECTOR-GENERAL FOR THE STATE
DIF - INTEGRAL FAMILY DEVELOPMENT
No. 6 CALLE PASTEUR
CASA DE ECALA
QUERETARO, QRO.

Esteemed Sir:

I, ALEJANDRO GONZALEZ DUQUE, Esq., of
legal age and married, in the capacity
of Deputy Attorney for the Defense of
Minors appointed by the National System for
Integral Family Development in the State
of San Luis Potosí, residing in Ciudad de
Valles, S.L.P., with all due respect submit
for your consideration and adjudication:
    With the objective that you might see
fit to direct to whom it may concern the
family matter I will outline in greater
detail below, as the person with whom we
should speak resides at Calle Arteaga 108
```

in downtown Querétaro, Qro., and expressing my gratitude in advance for your attention and prompt response to this matter, I present the facts of the situation:

I refer to the matrimony of ISIDORO URIBE LOPEZ and MARIA LILIA SANCHEZ PEREZ, a contract entered into by both parties on April the seventeenth, 1974, as documented by the facsimile of their marriage certificate, attached as Exhibit 1; the aforementioned matrimony produced two minors of the names XXXXXX XXXXXX URIBE SANCHEZ and SARA MARIA URIBE SANCHEZ. This family was dissolved in the year 1979 as a result of an attempt by the male spouse to liquidate his wife, by forcibly and with violence obliging her to ingest pesticide, pursuant to innumerable threats, beatings, and incidents of excessive cruelty. Following this event, one further attempt at cohabitation between late 1980 and early 1981 proved untenable and the couple separated definitively shortly thereafter. Mrs. MARIA LILIA SANCHEZ PEREZ died on September the sixth, 1989. Two years prior to her death, the health of this individual began to fail, which forced her to seek refuge in Ciudad de Valles, being the owner of a residence located at Calle de Galeana, across the street from the home of her brother, a man by the name of FERNANDO SANCHEZ PEREZ, with the intention of securing his protection for herself and her daughters. In light of their father's indifference, the minors were left in the care of the decedent's brother, who was provided a sum of money, the interest from which was to be used in the supplying all necessities to the minors, and so it was for a time as the minors developed, until the aforementioned began to manifest extreme rebelliousness, a lack of respect and an inattention to personal hygiene, and a distaste for the persons around them, etc.

Thereby, Mr. FERNANDO SANCHEZ PEREZ, charged with the guardianship of these minors, finds it beyond his means to control them and, subsequently, finds himself obliged to appeal to the Office of Social Assistance to manifest his prior attempt to enroll these youths in boarding school in order to instill in them some discipline, an attempt which ultimately failed, given that within twenty-four hours the minors created absolute chaos at said institution and were expelled. Mr. FERNANDO SANCHEZ PEREZ solicited our assistance with the objective of depositing the minors with their father, Mr. ISIDORO URIBE LOPEZ, and as such we kindly request that you review this matter for the purpose of reintegrating the minors with their father and, should it prove necessary, that all legal means be pursued toward the end of obligating the father to fulfill his paternal duties. We await your instructions regarding when to deposit the minors with the aforementioned individual.

With gratitude in advance for your collaboration, and at your disposal for similar cases, I remain, as ever, your faithful servant.

Sincerely,
ALEJANDRO GONZALEZ DUQUE
DEPUTY ATTORNEY FOR THE DEFENSE
OF MINORS

I'M ASHAMED TO admit that it was only late in life that I began to think about victims of femicide. The latest figures from Mexico's National Institute of Statistics and Geography suggest that 62.7 percent of women fifteen years or older have been the victims of at least one violent incident. And it wasn't until even later that I began to think about their bodies as an extension of my own, as bodies that are my/our concern. As I write this, seven women are murdered every day in Mexico.[1] In 1993, when I heard about femicides in Ciudad Juárez for the first time, I was about to turn fifteen, and that northern city with its dead women was a distant place, completely foreign; I didn't understand its connection to where I lived. I was unable to construct an ethical or affective relationship between those women's bodies and my own.

It was the so-called war on drugs that made me think about those bodies, to mourn those victims of violence, especially the women. One woman, in particular. An unidentified woman, found face down and naked on a bench, under a tree, with a rose on her back and a sign that appeared to be a message from a cartel. The photographs showed the body on site, cleaved impeccably at each of its joints: neck, shoulders, elbows, wrists, hips, knees, ankles. And then later, on a slab at the morgue, in an exact reproduction of how the body was arranged to be found. I don't know her name, but I thought and continue to think about this unknown woman, about the image of her body, taken apart and put back together.

---

1. Translator's note: At the time of translation, this statistic has risen— by conservative estimates—to ten women and girls murdered every day, not counting the murders of trans women, which are often intentionally misclassified.

"I didn't know that a woman could be killed for the sole fact of being a woman, but I've been hearing stories and, over time, I've begun to piece it together," writes Selva Almada in *Dead Girls*, introducing the cases of murdered and disappeared women that the Argentinean novelist traces, investigates, and dissects in sharp and mournful prose. "They never told us: You might be raped by your husband, your father, your brother, your cousin, your neighbor, your grandfather, your teacher. By the men you trust." By the men or by the state you trust. When you're growing up, no one tells you straight out: Your life is in danger, your existence is always under threat, in public spaces and in your own home, late at night or in the middle of the day, in any kind of clothing, with or without makeup; you risk being harassed, raped, kidnapped, trafficked, tortured, killed by strangers or by those closest to you, individuals who will, almost invariably, walk away unscathed. No one tells you: Your life is at risk because you are a woman.

TO WRITE THIS text, I had to go back to the document. I decided to transcribe it because I realized that each time I read it, it's like reading it for the first time. As if I hadn't read it well any of the previous times. As if I had unread it each time I got to the end.

The petition contains terms I think about obsessively. "Liquidate," for example. Why that verb, and not "kill" or "murder"? I consult the dictionary; it isn't until the ninth entry that the informal usage "to get rid of someone by killing them" appears. The tenth entry, also colloquial, reads "to end or suppress something, or to make it disappear."

"Excessive cruelty." By definition, the second word evokes inhumanity, atrocity. The first suggests the act of going too far, overstepping what is fair or reasonable. Why attach that adjective, that extra weight, to the noun? What did those two words mean, together, on my mother's body?

I WORKED IN the public sector for ten years. First as the director of a historical archive in Tampico, then as the director of cultural spaces at the Institute of Culture and the Arts in Tamaulipas. I know, firsthand, what goes on behind the closed doors of bureaucracy. Every petition, form, report, or memorandum is ignored unless there's follow-up from the person who wants to see the document's intended purpose carried out. I'm not talking about a simple phone call. If you want a payment to go through, a purchase made, or even just a poster designed for a cultural event, brace yourself: you'll need to ask not once, but five or ten times for whatever you already requested with a petition on official letterhead. When I was working in the historical archive, I remember needing to send an official request to my immediate supervisor every week for nearly two years to get them to check and replace our fire extinguishers. That's right: in a *historical archive.*

When Fernando died, there was no one to follow up on his petition, which probably remained among the active files for a while before being passed to the archive and eventually purged. It's ironic, however you look at it: the state's inefficiency saved us from the state. Even if we were to imagine Alejandro as a functionary with a strong sense of ethics and critical distance who would have determined that Isidoro was unfit to care for two little girls, he would have been obligated to send us to an orphanage or a DIF center. This would have implied an entirely different set of problems. Many who are sent to such institutions describe daily life there as a succession of harsh punishments and restrictions, not to mention physical and sexual violence.

In 2014, the story broke of a youth shelter called La Gran Familia in Zamora, Michoacán; it was a place for "lost causes" and orphans run by a woman known as "Mama Rosa" where countless crimes were committed, including the corruption of minors and unlawful deprivation of liberty, as well as physical, psychological, and sexual abuse. In 2017, I read the news about the forty-one teenage girls who died in a fire at the Virgen de la Asunción shelter for minors in San José Pinula, Guatemala; the institution was overseen by the Secretary of Social Welfare and femicide had been committed there. Reading about these cases, I couldn't help but think that one of those stories would have been mine if I had stayed at the boarding-school reformatory or been placed in a DIF orphanage.

Faced with the choice between suffering violence or death at the hands of my father and violence or death at the hands of the state, my best option was for the state to abandon me. To go unnoticed until I was no longer a minor. To grow up alone, without a guardian. To live on the margins of the state, in its cracks and dark corners. To run from it in order to survive.

WHEN THE ARGENTINEAN tourists Marina Menegazzo, twenty-one, and María José Coni, twenty-two, were sexually assaulted and murdered in Ecuador in 2016, all the headlines, news reports, tweets, and conversations about them said the two girls were traveling alone. Alone. As if they hadn't had each other. As if they hadn't had themselves. As if accompanied travel required more people. Men. A man. According to public sentiment, if a man had been traveling with them, they wouldn't have been traveling alone. But the fact of the matter is that they, like all women, are always alone—they are always unaccompanied by the state. As Cristina Rivera Garza might say, "Two women unaccompanied by the state on a highway along which the army advances."

> [My editor says I rush the ending. She's right. There should be a paragraph here that serves as a bridge, that channels the tension toward the essay's close. But I've been trying to come back to this text for the past two or three weeks, and I just can't. I don't want to see it again for a long time. Writing this broke me in ways I didn't expect. Daniela Rea says it would be a good idea to ask myself what the forty-year-old me hopes to interpellate in the twelve-year-old me. I read two definitions of interpellate: 1. To require, compel, or simply ask for an explanation or that an obligation be fulfilled; 2. To implore someone's aid in the form of support and protection. So, no. I'm not interpellating anyone, or anything, in the first sense of the word. There really isn't anyone to interpellate. Maybe, if I could, I'd just like to tell my mother and twelve-year-old Sara that they're not alone. Or rather, that they are, but they have themselves. To say this to them, and to myself, as well. I realize that the person I'm interpellating, in the second sense of the word, is me.]

Women unaccompanied by the state, searching for mothers, daughters, and sisters who have been taken; women seeking justice for their dead. Women unaccompanied by the state, joining other women unaccompanied by the state, piecing together networks and strategies to save, to interpellate, to support and protect themselves and each other, among themselves.

Zapatista Army for National Liberation
(EZLN)

LETTER FROM THE ZAPATISTA WOMEN TO WOMEN IN STRUGGLE AROUND THE WORLD[1]

1. Adapted by Gabriela Jauregui and Heather Cleary from the English translation available at enlacezapatista.ezln.org.mx.

SISTER, COMPAÑERA:

We Zapatista women send you our greetings as the women in struggle that we all are.

We have sad news for you today, which is that we are not going to be able to hold the Second International Encounter of Women in Struggle here in Zapatista territory in March of 2019.

Maybe you already know the reasons why, but if not, we'll tell you a little about them here:

The new bad governments have said clearly that they are going to carry forward the big capitalists' megaprojects, including the Tren Maya, their plan for the Tehuantepec Isthmus, and their massive commercial tree farms. They have also said that they'll allow the mining companies to come in, as well as agribusiness. On top of that, their agrarian plan is wholly oriented toward destroying us as Indigenous peoples by converting our lands into commodities, picking up where Carlos Salinas de Gortari left off when we stopped him with our uprising.

All of these are projects of destruction, no matter how they try to disguise them with lies, no matter how many times they multiply their thirty million votes. The truth is that they are coming for everything now, coming full force against Indigenous peoples, their communities, lands, mountains, rivers, animals, plants, even their rocks.

They are not just going to try and destroy us Zapatista women, but all Indigenous women—and all men for that matter. But here we're talking as and about women.

In their plans, our lands will no longer be for us but for the tourists and their big hotels and fancy restaurants and all of the businesses that make it possible for the tourists to have these luxuries.

They want to turn our lands into plantations for the production of lumber, fruit, and water, and into mines to extract gold, silver, uranium, and all of the minerals that the capitalists are after.

They want to turn us into their peons, into servants who sell our dignity for a few coins every month.

Those capitalists and the new bad governments who obey them think that what we want is money.

They don't understand that what we want is freedom, that even the little we have attained has been through our struggle, without any attention, without photos and interviews, without books or referendums or polls, and without votes, museums, or lies.

They don't understand that what they call "progress" is a lie, that they can't even provide safety for all of the women who continue to be beaten, raped, and murdered in their progressive or reactionary worlds.

How many women have been murdered in those progressive or reactionary worlds while you read these words, compañera, sister?

Maybe you already know this, but we'll tell you clearly that here in Zapatista territory, not a single woman has been

LETTER FROM THE ZAPATISTA WOMEN

murdered for many years. Can you imagine? And we're the ones they call backward, ignorant nothings.

Maybe we don't know which feminism is the best one, maybe we don't say "cuerpa" instead of "cuerpo," or however it is you change words around, maybe we don't know what "gender equity" is or any of those other things with too many letters to count. In any case, that concept of "gender equity" isn't even well-formulated because it only refers to women and men, and even we, supposedly ignorant and backward, know that there are those who are neither men nor women and we call them "otroas," though they call themselves whatever they feel like. It hasn't been easy for them to earn the right to be what they are without having to hide because they are mocked, persecuted, abused, and murdered. Why should they be obligated to be men or women, to choose one side or the other? We shouldn't disrespect their refusal to choose. How are we going to complain that we aren't respected as women if we don't respect these people? Maybe we think this way because we are just talking about what we've seen in other worlds, and we don't know a lot about these things.

What we do know is that we fought for our freedom and now we have to fight to defend it so that the painful history that our grandmothers suffered is not relived by our daughters and granddaughters.

We struggle so history isn't repeated and we don't return to a world where we only cook food and bear children, just to see them grow up into humiliation, disrespect, and death.

We didn't rise up in arms to return to the same thing.

We haven't been resisting for twenty-five years in order to end up serving tourists, bosses, and overseers.

We will not stop our work in the fields of education, health, culture, and media; we will not stop being autonomous authorities in order to become hotel and restaurant employees, serving strangers for a few pesos. It doesn't matter if it's a few pesos or many, what matters is that our dignity has no price.

Because that's what they want, compañera, sister: that we become slaves in our own lands, taking handouts in exchange for letting them destroy the community.

COMPAÑERA, SISTER:
When you came to these mountains for the 2018 gathering, we saw that you looked at us with respect, maybe even admiration. Not everyone did—we know that some only came to criticize us and look down on us. But that doesn't matter—the world is big and full of different kinds of thinking; some understand that not all of us can do the same thing, and some don't. We can respect that difference, compañera, sister, because that's not what the gathering was for, to see who would give us good reviews or bad reviews. It was to meet and understand each other as women who struggle.

Also, we do not want you to look at us now with pity or shame, as if we were servants taking orders delivered more or less politely, or as if we were vendors with whom to haggle over the price of their crafts or fruit and vegetables or whatever. Haggling is what capitalist women do, though of course when they go to the mall, they don't haggle over the price; they pay whatever the capitalist asks in full, and they do it happily.

No, compañera, sister. We're going to fight with all our strength and everything we've got against these mega-projects. If these lands are conquered, it will be by shedding the blood of us Zapatista women.

That is what we have decided and that is what we intend to do.

LETTER FROM THE ZAPATISTA WOMEN 301

It seems these new bad governments think that because we're women, we're going to promptly lower our gaze and obey the master and his new overseers. They think what we're looking for is a good boss and a good wage.

That's not what we're looking for. What we want is freedom, a freedom nobody can give us because we have to gain it ourselves with our struggle, with our own blood.

Do you think that when the new bad government's forces—its paramilitaries, its national guard—come for us we are going to greet them with respect, gratitude, and joy?

Hell no. We will greet them with a fight and then we'll see if they learn that Zapatista women don't give in, give up, or sell out.

Last year during the women's gathering, we made a great effort to ensure that you, compañera and sister, were happy and safe and joyful. Nevertheless, you left us a sizable pile of complaints: that the boards you slept on were hard, that you didn't like the food, that meals were expensive, that this or that should or shouldn't have been this way or that way. But we've already told you about our work to prepare the gathering and about the criticism we received.

What we want to tell you now is that even with all the complaints and criticisms, you were safe here: there were no bad men or even good men looking at you or judging you. It was all women here, you can attest to that.

Well now it's not safe anymore, because capitalism is coming for us, and it wants everything, no matter what. This assault is now possible because those in power feel that many people support them and will applaud them no matter what atrocities they carry out. What they're going to do is attack us and then check the polls to see if their ratings are still up, again and again until we have been annihilated.

Even as we write this letter, the paramilitary attacks have begun. They are the same groups as always—first they were with the PRI, then the PAN, then the PRD, then the PVEM, and now with MORENA.

So we are writing to tell you, compañera, sister, that we are not going to hold a women's gathering here, but you should do so in your lands, according to your times and ways.

Although we won't attend, you will be in our thoughts.

COMPAÑERA, SISTER:

Never stop your struggle. Even if those damned capitalists and their new bad governments get their way and annihilate us, you must keep struggling in your world.

That's what we agreed in the gathering: that we would all struggle so that no woman in any corner of the world would be afraid to be a woman.

Compañera, sister: your corner of the world is your corner in which to struggle, just like our struggle is here in Zapatista territory.

The new bad governments think that they will defeat us easily, that there are very few of us, and that nobody from any other world supports us.

But that's not the case, compañera, sister, because even if there is only one of us left, she's going to fight to defend our freedom.

We are not afraid, compañera, sister.

If we weren't scared twenty-five years ago when nobody even knew we existed, we certainly aren't going to be scared now that you have seen us—however you saw us, good or bad, you saw us.

LETTER FROM THE ZAPATISTA WOMEN

COMPAÑERA, SISTER:

Take care of that little light that we gave you.

Don't let it go out.

Even if our light here is extinguished by our blood, even if other lights go out in other places, take care of yours because even when times are difficult, we have to keep being what we are, and what we are is women in struggle.

That's all we wanted to say, compañera, sister. In summary, we're not going to hold a women's gathering here; we're not going to participate.

If you hold a gathering in your world and anyone asks you where the Zapatistas are and why didn't they come, tell them the truth: tell them we are fighting in our corner of the world for our freedom, as the Zapatista women we are.

That's all, compañeras, sisters, take care of yourselves.

We may not see each other again.

Maybe they'll tell you not to bother thinking about the Zapatistas anymore because we no longer exist. They'll tell you there are no more Zapatistas.

But just when you think they're right, that we've been defeated, you'll see that we still see you and one of us, without you even noticing, will come close and whisper, for only you to hear: "Where is the little light we gave you?"

From the mountains of the Mexican Southeast,
The Zapatista Women
February 2019

PERMISSIONS ACKNOWLEDGMENTS

"Feminism Without a Room of One's Own," Dahlia de la Cerda (tr. Julianna Neuhouser)

The excerpt from "It's the Poverty" is reprinted from Cherríe Moraga, "It's the Poverty." Copyright © 1981, 1983 by Cherríe Moraga. First published in 1981 in the Persephone Press edition of *This Bridge Called My Back: Writings by Radical Women of Color* (Fourth Edition, 2015 by SUNY Press) and in *Loving in the War Years* (South End Press, 1983). Used by permission of Stuart Bernstein Representation for Artists, New York, NY.

"I Am Hunger," Ytzel Maya (tr. Julia Sanches)

The excerpt from *Lesbian Peoples* is reprinted from Monique Wittig and Sande Zeig, *Lesbian Peoples: Material for a Dictionary.* Copyright © 1979 by Monique Wittig and Sande Zeig. Used by permission of Sande Zeig.

The excerpt from *The Lesbian Body* is reprinted from Monique Wittig, *The Lesbian Body*, translated by David LeVay. Copyright © 1973 by Monique Wittig, English translation copyright © 1975 by David LeVay. Used by permission of Winter Editions.

"While the Girls Are Asleep," Daniela Rea (tr. Gabriela Ramirez-Chavez)

The excerpts from *Empty Houses* are reprinted from Brenda Navarro, *Empty Houses*, translated by Sophie Hughes. Copyright © 2019 by Brenda Navarro, English translation copyright © 2021 by Sophie Hughes. Used by permission of Daunt Books.

The excerpts from *My Mother's Hands* are reprinted from Nellie Campobello, *Cartucho and My Mother's Hands*, translated by Doris Meyer and Irene Matthews. Copyright © 1938 by Nellie Campobello, English translation copyright © 1988 by Irene Matthews. Used by permission of the University of Texas Press.

The excerpts from *Contra los hijos* are reprinted from Lina Meruane, *Contra los hijos*. Copyright © 2014 by Lina Meruane. Used by permission of the author.

The excerpts from *Se llaman nebulosas* are reprinted from Maricela Guerrero, *Se llaman nebulosas*. Copyright © 2010 by Maricela Guerrero. Used by permission of the author.

"First Person Plural," Cristina Rivera Garza (tr. Heather Cleary)

The excerpts from "Agony Outside the Wall," "False Elegy," and "Meditations on the Threshold" are reprinted from Rosario Castellanos, *Poesía no eres tú*. Copyright © 1972 by Rosario Castellanos. The original poems "Falsa elegía," "Agonía fuera del muro," and "Meditación en el umbral" by Rosario Castellanos appear in Rosario Castellanos, *Poesía no eres tú*, 4ª ed., FCE, México, 2004, on pages 116, 179, and 328.

ABOUT THE CONTRIBUTORS

Yásnaya Elena A. Gil (Ayutla Mixe, 1981) is a scholar, writer, and activist who holds a master's degree in linguistics from UNAM and works to defend language rights. She was part of the "Power 100" list of most influential people in the contemporary art world by *ArtReview* magazine in 2021. She publishes regularly in *El País* and the Spanish edition of the *Washington Post* and is the author of the book *Ää: Manifiestos sobre la diversidad lingüística* (Almadía and Bookmate, 2020).

Marina Azahua (Mexico City, 1983) is a writer, editor, and translator with a bachelor's degree in history from UNAM, an MA in creative writing from the University of Melbourne in Australia, and a PhD in anthropology from Columbia University. Her work has been supported by numerous grants, including Mexico's National Fund for Culture and the Arts (FONCA) and the Foundation for New Ibero-American Journalism. She is one of five founding editors of the Mexican independent publishing house Ediciones Antílope.

Fernanda Latani M. Bravo (Oaxaca, 1991) is a Zapotec woman and feminist geographer; her second name, "Latani," carries within it her love and respect for the mountains. Over the course of her four years studying geography, she has constructed alternative processes in order to subvert how the subject is traditionally taught; she now employs these anticolonial, anticapitalist, antiracist, and antipatriarchal strategies in her own teaching. Her postgraduate work in feminist geographies focuses on the participation of indigenous women in resistance movements and political organizing in response to forced displacements and corporate megaprojects.

Pia Camil (Mexico City, 1980) earned a BFA from RISD and an MFA from the Slade School of Fine Art, London. She recently published her first monograph, *Friendly Fires*, with Inventory Press (2024). Her solo exhibitions include *Organismo Multi Orgásmico*, Sultana Galerie, Paris (2022); *Nidos y Nudos*, Blum & Poe Gallery, LA (2021); and *Laugh Now, Cry Later*, Galería OMR, CDMX (2020). Her museum and institutional solo shows include *Fuego Amigo*, Museo Carrillo Gil, Mexico City (2024); *ARS22*, Museum of Contemporary Art Kiasma, Helsinki (2022); *Air Out Your Dirty Laundry*, MASA at Rockefeller Center, New York (2022); and *Here Comes The Sun*, performance at Guggenheim Museum, New York (2019), among others. Camil's work is in the permanent collections of institutions including Centre Georges Pompidou in Paris, Museo Jumex in Mexico City, Blanton Museum of Art in Austin, the Guggenheim Museum in New York, and the FRAC Champagne-Ardenne in France. She lives and works between Acatitlán in the State of Mexico and Mexico City.

Dahlia de la Cerda (Aguascalientes, 1985) is a writer, activist, and philosopher. She is the author of the book *Medea me cantó un corrido* (Sexto Piso, 2024), the short story collection *Reservoir Bitches* (Feminist Press, 2024), translated from the

ABOUT THE CONTRIBUTORS

Spanish into multiple languages, and the essay collection *Desde los zulos* (Sexto Piso, 2022), and is codirector of the prochoice feminist organization Morras Help Morras.

Heather Cleary (New York, 1982) is an award-winning translator of poetry and prose whose work has been recognized by English PEN, the National Book Foundation, and the Mellon Foundation, among others. Her most recent works are *Recital of the Dark Verses* by Luis Felipe Fabre, *Reservoir Bitches* by Dahlia de la Cerda (cotranslated with Julia Sanches), and *Pink Slime* by Fernanda Trías. She has judged several national translation prizes, teaches at Sarah Lawrence College, and is the author of *The Translator's Visibility: Scenes from Contemporary Latin American Fiction* (Bloomsbury, 2021).

Alexandra R. DeRuiz (Mexico City, 1962) identifies as a transfeminine person. She is a teacher, translator, and author of the memoir *Crucé la frontera en Tacones* (Egales, 2023) and the essays appearing in the *Material de lectura* collection (UNAM, 2023). She is program director at La Jauría Trans, a virtual activism and support program for trans and gender-diverse people in Mexico City. She is also a freelance consultant and researcher in gender and sexuality. She has an AA in psychology from the City College of San Francisco and an English language teaching certification with the University of Dayton, completed the Trans Education and Training Assistance in Trans Health (TEACH) training in Bangkok, Thailand, and studied literature and writing at the University of El Claustro de Sor Juana in Mexico City. DeRuiz is an advocate for the human rights of trans migrants who transit through Mexico on their way to the border with the United States, trans sex workers, trans mature adults, and trans people living with HIV.

312   ABOUT THE CONTRIBUTORS

She provides workshops and cultural sensibility trainings on LGBTQI+ issues, organizing conferences and mobilizations internationally, including in Latin America, Europe, Asia, and Africa.

Lia García (Mexico City, 1989) is a teacher, writer, and performance artist; she is a feminist-in-training and a trans' activist. In 2016, she cofounded the Red de Juventudes Trans (Trans Youth Network) with Jessica Marjane, and in 2019 she established the archive of LGBTQIA+ children's and YA literature *Trans*Marikitas*.

Jimena González (Mexico City, 2000) is a writer and spoken-word poet and the author of *Todavía tiemblo*, her first poetry chapbook (momo room, 2020).

Gabriela Jauregui (Mexico City, 1979) is a writer, translator, and editor. She is the author of the novel *Feral* (Sexto Piso, 2022), winner of the Mexican National Fine Arts Award and finalist for the Amazon First Novel Prize; *Many Fiestas* (Gato Negro, 2017 and 2023); *Leash Seeks Lost Bitch* (Song Cave, 2016); and *Controlled Decay* (Akashic Books, 2008); as well as the short story collection *La memoria de las cosas* (Sexto Piso, 2015). She edited and coauthored the essay collections *Tsunami* (Sexto Piso, 2018) and *Tsunami 2* (2021), as well as *Tsunami 3* (2024). She is a Soros New American Fellow, a Borchard Fellow, and was selected as part of the Hay Festival's Bogotá 39 list of the thirty-six best young authors in Latin America. She is cofounder of the Aura Estrada Prize for young women writers, and lives and works in the forests belonging to the Mazahua peoples and the monarch butterflies.

ABOUT THE CONTRIBUTORS 313

Valeria Luiselli (Mexico City, 1983) has written books that have been translated into thirty languages and include (in English) *Sidewalks, Faces in the Crowd, The Story of My Teeth, Tell Me How It Ends: An Essay in Forty Questions,* and *Lost Children Archive.* Her work has twice been awarded the Los Angeles Times Book Prize and was twice shortlisted for the National Book Critics Circle Award. She is both a MacArthur and a Guggenheim Fellow.

Ytzel Maya (State of Mexico, 1993) is a writer and researcher. She holds a bachelor's degree in literature and a master's degree in political sociology. As a researcher, she has specialized in political economy and drug policy. Her essays and articles have been published in media outlets and magazines such as *Letras Libres, Animal Político, Nexos,* and *Tierra Adentro,* among others.

Brenda Navarro (Mexico City, 1982) is a novelist and screen-writer. Her first novel, *Empty Houses* (2019), was awarded the Tigre Juan Prize in Spain and has been translated into ten languages. Her second book, *Eating Ashes* (2022), won the Cálamo Prize and the Madrid Bookstore Association's Prize in 2022, and was a finalist for the Mario Vargas Llosa Biennial Novel Prize in 2023. It is being translated into eleven languages. In Fall 2023, she was a writer-in-residence in the International Writing Program at the University of Iowa.

Julianna Neuhouser (Bloomington, 1987) is an American-Mexican translator, antifascist researcher, and anarchatrans-feminist writer. Her previous translations have included Osvaldo Bayer, Sergio González Rodríguez, and Arqueles Vela, while

314   ABOUT THE CONTRIBUTORS

her essays and journalism have been published in outlets such as *Gatopardo*, *ZonaDocs*, Malvestida, Trans Safety Network, and *Revista Común*. She edited and cowrote *Polarization and Transphobia: Critical Perspectives on the Advance of Anti-Trans and Anti-Gender Movements in Mexico* (2023).

Jumko Ogata-Aguilar (Xalapa, 1996) is an AfroJapanese and pocha writer, translator, and antiracism educator. She holds a bachelor's degree in Latin American studies from the National Autonomous University of Mexico (UNAM). She has been published by the British Council of Mexico, *Revista de la Universidad de México*, and *Vogue* Mexico. She is the author of *Mi Pelo Chino*, a bilingual children's book published in Spanish and Mixtec that highlights the beauty of curly and kinky hair. Her work is included in *Daughters of Latin America*, edited by Sandra Guzmán (2023). She is the translator of the Spanish-language edition of bell hooks's *Sisters of the Yam* (2024). She has facilitated workshops on antiracism and AfroMexican history for Facebook, Twitter, and the Department of Culture of Mexico as well as nonprofit organizations in Mexico and the US.

Gabriela Ramirez-Chavez (Los Angeles, 1992) is a Seattle-based poet and translator born to Guatemalan immigrants. She holds a doctorate in literature and specializes in Indigenous literatures of Latin America, especially from Mesoamerica. Her translations have been featured on NPR and in *POETRY*, *World Literature Today*, *BOMB*, and *Daughters of Latin America: An International Anthology of Latine Women*, among other publications. Gabriela's own poetry has appeared in literary journals and anthologies including *The Wandering Song: Central American Writing in the United States*.

ABOUT THE CONTRIBUTORS 315

Daniela Rea (Irapuato, 1982) is an award-winning journalist and documentary filmmaker, author of *Nadie les pidió perdón: historias de impunidad y resistencia* (2016) and director of *No sucumbió la eternidad* (2017) and *Buscadores en un país de desaparecidos* (2017). She is the cofounder of Periodistas de a Pie, a collective of independent journalists that compiled the book *Entre las cenizas* (2012).

Cristina Rivera Garza (Matamoros, 1964) is an internationally celebrated writer, scholar, and translator; she was recently named a MacArthur Genius and is the only person to have been twice awarded the prestigious Sor Juana Inés de la Cruz Prize. Her work has been translated into many languages. Some of her works available in English include *The Iliac Crest* (2017), *The Taiga Syndrome* (2018), *Grieving* (2020), and *The Restless Dead* (2020), and most recently, *Liliana's Invincible Summer: A Sister's Search for Justice* (2023), a National Book Award finalist and *New York Times*, *Washington Post*, *Time*, and *New Yorker* Book of the Year.

Julia Sanches (São Paulo, 1987) translates literature from Spanish, Portuguese, and Catalan into English. She has been longlisted and shortlisted for several prizes, including the International Booker, the National Translation Award, and the Reina Sofía Prize, and was awarded the 2022 PEN Translation Prize for *Migratory Birds* by Mariana Oliver. Her most recent works are *Living Things* by Munir Hachemi, *Reservoir Bitches* by Dahlia de la Cerda (cotranslated with Heather Cleary), and *Mammoth* by Eva Baltasar. Born in São Paulo, Brazil, she currently resides in Providence, RI.

ABOUT THE CONTRIBUTORS

Diana J. Torres (Madrid, 1981) is the author of *Pornoterrorismo* and *Pucha potens*, an anecdotal and scholarly study of female ejaculation. She owns a bar and is an activist and radical performance artist who lives and works in Mexico City.

Sara Uribe (Querétaro, 1978) is a poet and essayist who explores the relationship between poetry, body, ethics, and politics. Her most recent books include *Rosario Castellanos: materia que arde, Un montón de escritura para nada*, and *Antígona González*. Her work has been translated into English, Norwegian, Dutch, German, French, and Portuguese. Uribe has conducted creative writing workshops and worked as a university professor in academic writing and literature. She has been awarded two national poetry prizes in Mexico and is currently a member of the Sistema Nacional de Creadores de México.

The Zapatista Women have been part of the rank and file of the Zapatista Army for National Liberation (EZLN) from its inception, while the movement was still underground. During the uprising on January 1, 1994, as the EZLN made itself known to the world, the comandantas read the Ley Revolucionaria de Mujeres over the radio for all to hear. The document, written years before the Mexican state enacted any such laws, defends women's rights to live free from violence and decide autonomously over their bodies. Their actions also changed Indigenous women's participation in politics throughout the country and transformed the conversation in feminist circles nationwide. The comandantas have been clear all along: there is no liberation, no revolution, without women. This is not a performative slogan but rather an active form of organizing and world creating. For this first encuentro (gathering) of women in the struggle, they welcomed thousands of women into Zapatista territory for three days to discuss, imagine, and create a different world together in the autonomous territory known as "Torbellino de nuestras palabras" (Whirlwind of Our Words) in Morelia, Chiapas. More information about the Zapatista movement and the women's encuentros is available at https://enlacezapatista.ezln.org.mx/.

More Translated Literature from the Feminist Press

Bad Seed by Gabriel Carle,
translated by Heather Houde

**Blood Feast: The Complete
Short Stories of Malika Moustadraf**
translated by Alice Guthrie

**Grieving: Dispatches from a
Wounded Country**
by Cristina Rivera Garza,
translated by Sarah Booker

Happy Stories, Mostly
by Norman Erikson Pasaribu,
translated by Tiffany Tsao

Human Sacrifices by María Fernanda Ampuero,
translated by Frances Riddle

In Case of Emergency by Mahsa Mohebali,
translated by Mariam Rahmani

Panics by Barbara Molinard,
translated by Emma Ramadan

Reservoir Bitches by Dahlia de la Cerda,
translated by Heather Cleary and Julia Sanches

The Singularity by Balsam Karam,
translated by Saskia Vogel

Tongueless by Lau Yee-Wa,
translated by Jennifer Feeley

Violets by Kyung-Sook Shin,
translated by Anton Hur

The Feminist Press publishes books that ignite movements and social transformation. Celebrating our legacy, we lift up insurgent and marginalized voices from around the world to build a more just future.

See our complete list of books at
feministpress.org